KENNIKAT PRESS SCHOLARLY REPRINTS

Dr. Ralph Adams Brown, Senior Editor

Series on

ECONOMIC THOUGHT, HISTORY AND CHALLENGE

Under the General Editorial Supervision of

Dr. Sanford D. Gordon

Professor of Economics, State University of New York

THE UNITED STATES IN THE ORIENT

THE NATURE OF THE ECONOMIC PROBLEM

BY

CHARLES A. CONANT

KENNIKAT PRESS
Port Washington, N. Y./London

THE UNITED STATES IN THE ORIENT

First published in 1900
Reissued in 1971 by Kennikat Press
Library of Congress Catalog Card No: 72-137936
ISBN 0-8046-1441-5

Manufactured by Taylor Publishing Company Dallas, Texas

KENNIKAT SERIES ON ECONOMIC THOUGHT, HISTORY AND CHALLENGE

CONTENTS

PREFACE

The United States have recently assumed serious responsibilities in the Orient. While the manner of their assumption had something of the appearance of accident, this country has only followed other civilized states in the general movement to find outlets for their surplus capital and the products of their labor. The United States have actually reached, or are approaching, the economic state where such outlets are required outside their own boundaries, in order to prevent business depression, idleness, and suffering at home. Such outlets might be found without the exercise of political and military power, if commercial freedom was the policy of all nations. As such a policy has not been adopted by more than one important power of western Europe, and as the opportunities for the sale of the products of

American labor and the investment of American capital under conditions of equality of opportunity are seriously threatened by the policy of some of these powers, the United States are compelled, by the instinct of self-preservation, to enter, however reluctantly, upon the field of international politics.

The present volume does not undertake to discuss all aspects of our position in the Orient. It is concerned chiefly with the economic aspects of the subject, and not with its ethical or political aspects. Upon the ethical side, of the right of a higher civilization to extend its sovereignty at the expense of a weaker one, volumes have been written, and will continue to be written. It seems sufficient to note here that the English-speaking races are preëminently practical rather than severely logical. They do not permit themselves to be carried by a syllogism to extreme conclusions. The argument made by our fathers more than a century ago in favor of "the consent of the governed" was not meant by them to include universal suffrage, or to exclude sovereignty over annexed territory. This is the stubborn testimony of their acts. Reduced to its real meaning in the minds of the men who uttered it, their declaration meant that self-government should not be denied to those who were competent to exercise it for their own benefit and that of society. The attempt to read into their words meanings which they did not bear in the minds of those who uttered them, in order to carry an abstract theory to a merciless conclusion, after the manner of the philosophers of the French Revolution, is not in accordance with the sober adaptability to conditions as they find them which has ever marked the historic progress of the English-speaking peoples. American liberty, like English liberty, has been a plant of slow growth. It is not adapted to being torn up by the roots and transplanted in its entirety to foreign soil. The government of the United States, in seeking to establish orderly government in the Philippine Islands, with the limitations which grow out of conditions as they are, and refusing to make promises for future generations, which might not be fulfilled, would seem to be pursuing a wiser course than to expect the people of those islands to set up an ideal republic on a soil where even local self-government has hardly taken root, and where the sanctions of order and justice which promote industrial development are scarcely understood.

This problem of new markets, and the author's discussion of it, has sometimes been represented as a problem of capital and not of labor; but it is in fact of vital interest for the American laborer. Labor is perhaps more directly concerned than capital that new markets and new opportunities for investment should be found to relieve the congestion of the old markets. The question is not whether American laborers can find opportunities for work under the tropical sun of the Orient, but whether they shall find such opportunities at home by the maintenance of adequate markets abroad for absorbing their great product of finished goods and saved capital. Only by keeping such markets open can these products be sold upon conditions which will keep labor steadily employed, afford encouragement for additional production, and open new fields of employment. A large demand for labor, whether for completing finished goods for sale abroad or for preparing the machinery of production and transportation for the development of backward countries, will react upon wages by compelling competing employers to bid for labor in a market where it is scarce, instead of choosing between the minimum bids of idle laborers competing under conditions disturbed by overproduction at home and closed markets abroad.

Upon the side of capital itself, the laborer is also interested, since he is one of the largest contributors to the great fund of savings which seek investment in remunerative enterprises. It is more important to him, so long as the present structure of society is preserved, that capital should yield high and safe returns, than it is to the speculator on the stock exchange or the owner of inherited wealth. The thrifty laborer abroad, as well as in the United States, has become a capitalist whose savings suffer by the fall in the rate of interest, and will be permanently impaired in value, if he permits the markets of the world to be closed to the products of his labor.

Upon the administrative side, there is doubtless much to criticise in the conduct of all governing countries in their relations with weaker rivals or their own dependencies. But administrative errors, however deserving of censure they may be, seldom reverse economic tendencies. Whatever the merits of the ethical and political arguments which divide parties in the United States, the struggle, in which all the civilized nations are taking part, for colonial possessions and for new markets, indicates an economic problem of a serious character, which should be discussed without passion and solved without prejudice. They are not "traitors" who are convinced that expansion is unwise, and can give reasons for their belief; they are not without ethical ideals who believe that upon both the economic and moral side the application of American enterprise to our possessions in the East and of American civic standards to their future government will have benefits of a high character and wide scope for the United States and her island wards. To the discussion of this last phase of the subject, this book is a contribution.

The various chapters herewith presented appeared originally as magazine articles at intervals during the past two years, which will account for their form and for occasional repetitions. The author is indebted to the publishers of the "North American Review," "The Forum," and the "Atlantic Monthly," for permission to use the articles in book form. A list of the original articles appears at the back of the book. They have been changed in only trifling respects, where the language seemed capable of improvement, or slight omissions could be made without breaking the thread of the argument.

CHARLES A. CONANT.

BOSTON, September 25, 1900,

THE UNITED STATES IN THE ORIENT

I

THE ECONOMIC BASIS OF IMPERIALISM

THE instinctive tendency of a race or civilization often outruns the wisdom of its leaders. Whether for good or ill, the inborn tendencies of race — whether for the highest achievement in art, like the Ionian; the military conquest of the world, like the Roman; the penetration of distant and barbarous countries for the purposes of trade, like the Tyrian or the Venetian; the command of the empire of the sea, like the English — these tendencies prevail by a sort of instinct. Other races in seeking to pursue the same paths by imitation have stumbled and gone astray. But when the current of race or national tendencies runs strongly in a given channel, it is apt to override alike the misgivings of its sympathizers and the protests and resistance of those who would obstruct it. The United States to-day seem about to enter upon a path marked out for them as the children of the Anglo-Saxon race, not yet traversed because there has been so much to do at home. Almost as if by magic, the importance of naval power as the advance agent of commercial supremacy has flashed upon the mind of the country. The irresistible tendency to expansion, which leads the growing tree to burst every barrier, which drove the Goths, the Vandals, and finally our Saxon ancestors in successive and irresistible waves over the decadent provinces of Rome, seems again in operation, seeking new outlets for American capital and new opportunities for American enterprise.

This new movement is not a matter of sentiment. It is the result of a natural law of economic and race development. The great civilized peoples have to-day at their command the means of developing the decadent nations of the world. These means, in their material aspects, consist of the great excess of saved capital which is the result of machine production. It is proposed to point out in this chapter how great this excess is at the present time, how profoundly it is disturbing economic conditions in the older countries, and how necessary to the salvation of these countries is an outlet for their surplus savings, if the entire fabric of the present economic order is not to be shaken by a social revolution. The law of self-preservation, as well as that of the survival of the fittest, is urging our people on in a path which is undoubtedly a departure from the policy of the past, but which is inevitably marked out by the new conditions and requirements of the present.

The dominant note of modern economic life, since the beginning of the epoch of machinery and of negotiable securities, has been saving for investment. Saving against the risks of loss and the weakness of old age has existed from the beginning of civilization, and has been accompanied by a limited amount of saving for increasing the means of production. But saving for the sake of an income without the impairment of the principal is, in its present extension, a modern phenomenon. Savings had to be made, before the period of negotiable securities, in consumable commodities, in land and its improvements, or in metal, the great store of value. The creation of corporations and the issue of their shares in the form of securities afforded an outlet, toward the close of the last century and early in the present century, for savings which were becoming congested, because they could not be put to ready use.

The change in the form of the investment was only an evolution from the great demands for capital which arose with the application of machinery to production upon a large scale and the discovery of methods of communication on land and sea by the use of steam. The necessity for carrying on such large enterprises as cotton mills, iron foundries, and canal, railway, and steamship building by great aggregate sums of capital led to the conversion of the cost of the enterprise into divisible parts, which might absorb the savings of great numbers of men. For many years there was an outlet at a high rate of return for all the savings of all the frugal persons in the great civilized countries. Frightful miscalculations were made and great losses occurred, because experience had not gauged the value or the need of new works under all conditions, but there was room for the legitimate use of all savings without loss, and in enterprises affording an adequate return.

The conditions of the early part of the century have changed. Capital is no longer needed in excess of the supply, but it is becoming congested. The benefits of saving have been inculcated with such effect for many decades that savings accumulate beyond the development of new demands for capital which are legitimate, and are becoming a menace to the economic future of the great industrial countries. Jean Baptiste Say, the French economist, demonstrated by plausible reasoning that there could not be a general overproduction of commodities, because the increased product of one man or set of men would be exchanged against the increased product of the other producing classes of the community. But there was one flaw in this argument. M. Say based his reasoning upon the premise that the man who produced consumed in equal ratio with his production. He did not allow for saving. Saving is the setting aside from the products of one's labor or services of a portion of the proceeds for some other purpose than consumption. If every man in the community spent his entire income upon consumable goods, there would be no overproduction except as a result of mistaken adjustments. There could not be universal overproduction until every human being had more than he could consume or enjoy. But if every man should undertake to set aside a fixed proportion of the products of his labor for some other purpose than consumption, he would necessarily diminish the demand for the other classes of commodities which he had formerly obtained in exchange for his own products.

The answer of the economist to this proposition may be that savings, in their turn, are applied to furnishing the means of consumption to laborers. This is true so long as these laborers can be employed upon productive work. But, by the hypothesis, they must be employed upon some permanent work, like increasing the machinery of production or the means of communication. If these improvements are necessary, they pay an adequate return, and the point of congestion of capital has not been reached. If they are needless duplications of what already exists, they may either fail to pay dividends, or they may divide the work and earnings of the old machinery and laborers, making their creation barren of benefits to the community. In either case the person making the savings would have profited as much if he had applied his surplus to the purchase of consumable goods and luxuries, and the community would not have suffered by the employment of laborers in the production of such goods, in preference to their employment in the needless duplication of existing plant, destined to increase the inconveniences of overproduction, lock-outs, strikes, and commercial convulsions.

The famous proposition of John Stuart Mill that "Demand for commodities is not demand for labor" is true in a restricted sense, but, in the language of Professor Paul Leroy-Beaulieu, "has, in modern societies as they are constituted to-day, and with the enormous resources at their disposal, only a theoretical value." As M. Leroy-Beaulieu goes on to declare, "Circulating and available capital is exorbitantly abundant in all the old and rich societies." Mill's argument in its last analysis comes to this — that time is required between the consumption of saved commodities by laborers and the production by them of finished goods, and that consumption of commodities does not add to existing capital. These two propositions are theoretically true, but the element of time for preliminary saving has been substantially eliminated by modern conditions, and the evil of consuming commodities without saving has long ceased to be a threatening one. That a continuous demand for consumable commodities does constantly provide the capital for continuing their production is practically admitted by Mill when he says, in referring to a sudden cessation of demand for velvets, that the true test of his principle is "to suppose that the change is gradual and foreseen, *and is attended with no waste of capital.*"

If saving in any community no more than kept pace with new demands for capital which proved legitimate and profitable, the happy situation of a constantly progressive industrial condition would be realized. Saving is applied in too many cases, however, to the reproduction of machinery which is already sufficient and the creation of enterprises which do not prove productive. A few of these enterprises may do good to the community in the long run, by that process of friction which finally brings sound adjustments, but it can only be at the sacrifice of the savings of the first investors. It is the rude process of these readjustments which has lain beneath the intensity of economic crises during the present century. Some of these crises have been accompanied by delusions growing out of the novelty of the principle of limited liability and negotiable securities, which have added to their severity, but they have been due in an increasing degree in recent years to the vain seeking for safe investments which could not be found. The needless duplication of plant, the multiplication of unprofitable enterprises, has flooded the market with products which could hardly be consumed if all the means of the community were applied to consumption, and which have resulted, under the existing system of abstinence from consumption for the sake of saving, in a glut of goods which has destroyed profits, bankrupted great corporations, and ruined investors.

It is the excess of saving, with the resulting accumulation of unconsumed goods, in the great industrial countries, which is one of the world maladies of the economic situation of to-day. It lies at the root of a large share of industrial discontent, and explains more logically than changes in the mere mechanism of exchange the conditions which set in about 1870, when the great civilized countries first appear to have become fully capitalized to meet all demands for consumable goods which consumers were willing to make out of their earnings. The world's economic history since that time — the intense industrial activity in machine production and railroad building up to 1873; the long period of stagnation which followed, broken only by brief periods of activity after surplus goods had been consumed; the great accumulations of both capital and metallic money; the convulsions attacking the great capitalistic countries, without respect for their differences in tariff policies and money standards; and the steady fall in the earning power of capital — all these tendencies point to excess of saved capital beyond the effective demand of the community as their underlying cause. There must always be savings in a progressive industrial society to repair the wear of existing equipment and to meet new demands, but under the present social order it is becoming impossible to find at home in the great capitalistic countries employment for all the capital saved which is at once safe and remunerative.

The rapidity of savings and the extent of the congestion of capital in Europe may be judged from the stock exchange lists and the savings bank returns. In Great Britain the market value of the securities quoted on the stock exchange on June 18, 1898, was £3,215,414,000. In France the nominal and actual value of negotiable securities has recently been carefully worked out in a series of articles by M. Edmond Théry, the accomplished editor of "l'Economiste Européen." He shows that the market value of securities issued by French companies increased from $9,000,000,000 on July 1, 1890, to $13,250,000,000 on July 1, 1897, and while one tenth of this amount was held in each case abroad, this is offset four times over by foreign securities held in France. The market value of all securities held by Frenchmen, which was $11,000,000,000, paying an annual income of $480,000,000 in 1880, had risen in 1897 to $17,000,000,000, paying an annual income of $580,000,000. In this form of wealth alone, therefore, there has been an increase of more than 50 per cent. in capital in seventeen years, with an increase of less than 21 per cent. in money earnings. A part of this increase may be fictitious, in the sense that former private undertakings have been turned into stock companies, and that some of the stock companies represent worthless enterprises. The essential point, however, is not materially impaired, that the available money credits have been found among French investors to absorb this vast amount of stock in national, railway, and industrial securities. This increase, moreover, is a net increase in both nominal and market values, and takes account of the millions which have been sunk in worthless enterprises, like the Panama Canal, only at their capitalization and actual market value at the present time, and not at their issue value.

A calculation of all the movable wealth of leading European countries was undertaken in 1895 by the International Statistical Institute, under the direction of M. Alfred Neymarck, which covered the precious metals, mortgages, and savings deposits, as well as negotiable securities. The total was found to be about $85,000,000,000. M. Neymarck distributes this negotiable wealth among the various countries as follows: —

England	$35,000,000,000
Germany	18,000,000,000
France	15,500,000,000
Russia	5,000,000,000
Austria	4,500,000,000
The Netherlands	2,600,000,000
Italy	3,400,000,000
Belgium	1,200,000,000
Denmark	550,000,000
Roumania	240,000,000
Norway	150,000,000

In the four great investing countries of France, Germany, Austria-Hungary, and Great Britain, there are more than $46,000,000,000 of capital invested in negotiable securities alone — an amount nearly equal to forty times the bonded debt of the United States, and to $3250 for every family of five persons in the United States.

The statistics of the savings banks indicate in some degree the manner in which the common people have come to the aid of the great capitalists in accumulating loanable credit. The postal savings banks alone showed deposits, at recent dates, in Great

Britain and Ireland of $500,000,000; in France, $150,000,000; in Belgium, $100,000,000; in Italy, $90,000,000, and in Russia, $123,000,000. The French savings banks outside the postal service carry deposits to the amount of $650,000,000; the Swiss banks have $175,000,000, and the British trustee savings banks have $500,000,000. In these few countries, therefore, is an investment fund of nearly $2,500,000,000, derived from the savings of people of small means. In the United States the deposits in the savings banks in 1870 were $549,874,358, computed in depreciated paper money. In 1880 the amount, upon a gold valuation, was $819,106,973; in 1890, $1,524,844,506, and in 1897, $1,939,376,035. The amount has more than doubled during the fifteen years since 1882, when it stood at $966,797,081, and is equal to $26.56 for each man, woman, and child in the United States.

No account is taken of the deposit accounts of the great discount banks, because they grow largely out of current commercial transactions rather than new savings. These accounts could not exist without preliminary saving, but the capital which they represent corresponds rather to the circulating capital which maintains production than to the great funds which are seeking investment in new enterprises.

An essential question regarding this vast mass of accumulated saving invested in negotiable securities is whether it is put to profitable use. It is growing at a rate which would mean greatly increased prosperity in every country, if increase of savings were accompanied by increase of earning power in the old proportions. The statements compiled annually by M. Laveleye, the editor of the "Moniteur des Interêts Matériels" of Brussels, puts the total issues of new securities in 1897, including public loans, as well as railway and industrial stocks and bonds, at $1,800,000,000. This is considerably less than in 1896, when the issues were $3,200,000,000, but the conversions at that time were $1,500,000,000, as compared with only $135,000,000 in 1897, so that the net issues of new securities were not far apart in either year and amounted to nearly $1,800,000,000. The total for 1897 includes $26,000,000 in the United States and about the same amount in Canada, but the bulk was European capital, even where the recorded issues were in other countries. The applications of new capital to joint stock companies and security issues in Great Britain in 1897 were $775,000,000, and the issues of French securities in 1897 were computed by "l'Economiste Européen" of December 31, 1897, at $90,000,000.

The effect of these great accumulations of capital was predicted as long ago as 1879 by Professor Leroy-Beaulieu, the eminent French economist, in the first edition of his book, "Essai sur la Repartition des Richesses." He made it plain that if European laborers and capitalists continued to pile up savings in later years as they had already done up to that time, the supply of loanable capital would become so great that its earning power would be materially reduced. The continued tendency in this direction has been pointed out in a striking manner by Professor Leroy-Beaulieu himself and by M. Théry, in the series of articles already referred to, and is no longer a subject of dispute among European financiers. The conclusive evidence of the plenitude of capital and the cheapness of money is afforded by the conversions of the public debt which have been steadily going on among the great powers. Great Britain refunded her consolidated debt in 1888, and British consols now pay but little more than two per cent. at the current quotations. France negotiated loans of $880,000,000 between 1880 and 1890, most of which were issued at three per cent., but were quoted at only 85 to 91 per cent. up to 1890. Since then the quotations have steadily risen, until the real return in interest is summed up by M. Théry in the declaration that a capitalist who should have invested 10,000 francs in proportionate purchases of the six types of French national securities would have drawn from his investment in 1880 an annual revenue of 380 francs, in 1890, 355 francs, and in 1897 only 297 francs.

The great Prussian conversion was operated during 1897, and applied to $850,000,000 of consolidated four per cent. securities. These four per cents. were quoted at 104.5, and the three and a half per cents. were quoted at 104.2 in October, 1896. The three per cent. obligations issued in 1890 and then quoted at 86.5 reached par on July 5, 1895, and stood at 99.6 on October 5, 1896. One of the reasons for the close approximation of the four per cents. to the three and a half per cent. securities was the conviction that the government would soon proceed to the conversion of the former. M. Miquel, the Prussian Minister, in announcing his project, recalled the fact that in 1894 France had converted her four and a half per cents. into three and a half per cents.; that Sweden, Norway, Luxembourg, Zurich, Saxe-Gotha, Würtemberg, and Bavaria had converted four per cent. into three and a half per cent. securities; and that Denmark, Belgium, Holland, Bremen, and Berne had converted three and a half per cents. into three per cents., not to speak of the great Russian conversion of five per cents. into four per cents.

Figures like these illustrate in a forcible manner the superabundance of loanable capital in Europe and the small return which it now pays to investors. The evidence that the leading European states, in reducing their interest rates, have only followed the tendency of commercial loans is afforded by M. Théry in his discussion of railway and industrial securities. That the situation is on the point of becoming much worse for investors is indicated by the fact that not only are governments preparing for conversions of the public debt at reduced rates of interest, but some of the railways and industrial societies are preparing to pay off their obligations and narrow the field of possible investment. The leading railway companies of France are beginning to issue obligations at two and a half per cent., which are still quoted a little below par, but which, after the deduction of the tax upon corporation earnings and the tax upon transfers, pay a net return of only 2.44 per cent. a year. Of the French railway obligations 121,525,000 francs mature in 1900, 167,205,200 francs in 1910, 216,214,000 in 1920, and larger sums during the three succeeding decades.

This congestion of capital in Europe follows a distinct economic law. This law, as worked out by the eminent Austrian economist, Böhm-Bawerk, applies to the earnings of capital the law of diminishing returns. In other words, capital becomes less productive in earning power where it is abundant, because less productive use can be found for the excess above a certain limit. And it is this excess which fixes the rate for all. In the language of M. Leroy-Beaulieu, "The circumstance which most influences the rate of interest in civilized countries, where capital is generally sought and loaned for productive works, is the average productiveness of capital newly formed and the prospect of productiveness of capital which is available." Saving has reached a point in old countries where the offers of capital have almost exceeded the effective demand, and the owners of capital are bidding recklessly against each other for the purchase at high premiums of the evidences of the public debt and other unquestionable securities.

A remarkable proof that this great accumulation of capital is to a large extent doubling upon itself by duplicating the machinery of production, without substantial benefits to the community or even to investors, is afforded by the statistics of the French tax upon the income of negotiable securities. An article in "l'Economiste Français" of May 21, 1898, calls attention to the fact that the product of this tax, if the rates had been uniform, would show no appreciable increase for the past fifteen years. The rate was changed from three to four per cent. in 1891, so that the gross yield was increased, but the product of each one per cent. of the tax was 16,075,000 francs in 1883, and only 15,737,000 francs in 1896. This tax is levied upon the dividends paid upon negotiable securities.

If the fact that the yield of the tax had not increased were considered by itself, it would indicate that the increased savings of the French people and their large investments in negotiable securities for the past fifteen years had been absolutely barren of increased earning power. In other words, the superfluity of capital has so reduced dividends that all the additional savings of half a generation have no more than offset the effect of declining interest rates. This calculation is, of course, subject to qualification, by reason of large investments by Frenchmen in foreign securities which do not pay this tax, and by reason of the reduction in the prices of commodities, which increases the purchasing power of the dividends earned. But even with these qualifications, there could hardly be a more striking demonstration of the barrenness to the investor of the vast volume of modern savings and the manner in which the increase in volume accentuates the difficulty of sufficient savings to afford productive dividends.

The restlessness of capital under diminished earnings has been illustrated in many ways during the last few years. In every great capitalistic country there is an eager reaching out for new investments, which is sometimes willing to assume great risks rather than accept small returns. Germany, which was a comparatively poor country until within the present generation, is expanding greatly her foreign investments, in spite of occasional deficiencies of circulating capital at home. The proof that German capital is finding its way all over the world is found in the extension of German banks, of which there is one, with a capital of 10,000,000 marks ($2,500,000), in Brazil; one with head offices at Buenos Ayres and Valparaiso, with a capital of 20,000,000 marks; one at Shanghai and Calcutta, with a capital of 15,000,000 marks; and the German Bank of Chile, at Valparaiso, with a capital of 10,000,000 marks. Germany is interested in the Brazilian Railway of Minas, with a capital of 62,000,000 marks, and in the railways of Anatolia (which are almost wholly owned in Germany), with a capital of 26,720,000 marks and loans of 68,340,000 marks. German capital is also largely invested in breweries, paper mills, soap factories, textile mills, and machine shops in the United States.

Even Scotland, the example for many years of conservatism in banking and investments, has felt the pressure of the low returns upon saved capital in recent years. The Scotch incorporated banks gave notice on October 1, 1892, that after that date the allowance of interest on creditor balances of current accounts would be discontinued. This did not apply to distinct deposit accounts, but the rate on these was then only one and a half per cent., and was reduced in January, 1895, to one per cent. The congestion of capital in Scotland had already led to large transfers of money to Australia, and when the crisis of 1893 occurred in that country, about one third of the deposits of £153,000,000 were owned in Great Britain, chiefly in Scotland, and had been deposited in the Australian banks because of the liberal rate of interest paid.

The present situation in regard to saving is not absolutely novel in the world's experience. The Florentine cities found capital accumulating on their hands beyond the capacity for its safe employment, and were compelled to make precarious loans to foreign kings. Holland faced a congestion of capital in the days of her great maritime supremacy, when money sought investment in vain at two per cent., and the wild folly of the tulip mania illustrated the tendency to speculation which such conditions foster. England was afflicted with such a congestion of capital in the early days of the Stuarts, when prosperity and commercial greatness began to afford small business savings to Englishmen, and again in the middle of the last century, when three per cents. were quoted at 107. In each of these cases the world was far from rich, and savings could not be said to exist in excess in the sense that there was more than enough for all. But the question of congested capital is a practical one and not a sentimental one. The few who then saved, the many who save now, will not hand over their whole savings to the needy, except under compulsion of taxation, or under the cruel stress of an economic crisis which wipes out dividends and shrivels the value of investments.

There are three important solutions of

this enormous congestion of capital in excess of legitimate demand. One of these is the socialistic solution of the abandonment of saving, the application of the whole earnings of the laborer to current consumption, and the support of old age out of taxes levied upon the production of the community. It will be long before this solution will be accepted in a comprehensive form in any modern civilized state. The second solution is the creation of new demands at home for the absorption of capital. This has occurred at several previous stages of the world's history, and is likely to continue as long as human desires continue expansible. But there has never been a time before when the proportion of capital to be absorbed was so great in proportion to possible new demands. Means for building more bicycle factories than are needed, and for laying more electric railways than are able to pay dividends, have been taken out of current savings within the last few years, without producing any marked effect upon their amount, and without doing more, at the most, than to stay the downward course of the rate of interest. Aside from the waste of capital in war, which is only a form of consumption, there remains, therefore, as the final resource, the equipment of new countries with the means of production and exchange.

It is in the countries which Lord Salisbury describes as decaying that the means for the employment of new capital must be found. Western Europe and the Atlantic coast of the United States, with many of the interior States, are already fully equipped with the necessary means of production and communication. There remain many improvements of a permanent character capable of being made in the luxuries of living, but they are not in the nature of additions to the machinery of production and exchange. Such an improvement, for instance, would be the abolition of grade crossings by costly tunnels and bridges where the improvement obviously would not pay for itself, but was rendered possible out of the abundant surplus savings in the form of earnings of the railway or the State. These improvements are very desirable additions to the accumulated comforts of a community, but their creation is essentially in the nature of the employment of capital for consumption where they have no visible and appreciable effect upon earning capacity, rather than its employment as an investment. A railway which saw fit to employ a large surplus of earnings in such improvements would be pursuing the same course as an individual who applied his surplus to the purchase of valuable works of art and jewels. They would both have a permanent character, but not a productive character. The railway would not issue new interest-bearing securities for sale to investors for such purposes, and the individual would not borrow the savings of others and pay interest upon them, in order to add to his personal luxuries.

For the means of finding new productive employments for capital, therefore, it is necessary that the great industrial countries should turn to countries which have not felt the pulse of modern progress. Such countries have yet to be equipped with the mechanism of production and of luxury, which has been created in the progressive countries by the savings of recent generations. They have not only to obtain buildings and machinery, — the necessary elements in producing machine-made goods, —

but they have to build their roads, drain their marshes, dam their rivers, build aqueducts for their water supplies and sewers for their towns and cities. Asia and Africa are the most promising of these countries. Japan has already made her entry, almost like Athene full-armed from the brain of Zeus, into the modern industrial world. The increased capacity of her people for production, giving them increased command over the products of other peoples, is producing its natural effect in the rise of wages and increased importations. China, Siberia, and the islands which have languished so long under Spanish inertia, are likely to follow, perhaps with more halting steps, in the footsteps of Japan. The opening of railways and canals will afford employment for the masses of capital piling up in Europe and the United States, which will be profitable if the merchandise is found to feed the new means of transportation. Existing commodities now imported from the interior of these countries at great cost will be swept on paths of steel to the sea-coast, with the result of reducing their cost, increasing their consumption, and benefiting at once both producer and purchaser.

The United States cannot afford to adhere to a policy of isolation while other nations are reaching out for the command of these new markets. The United States are still large users of foreign capital, but American investors are not willing to see the return upon their investments reduced to the European level. Interest rates have greatly declined here within the last five years. New markets and new opportunities for investment must, therefore, be found, if surplus capital is to be profitably employed.

In pointing out the necessity that the United States shall enter upon a broad national policy, it need not be determined in just what manner that policy shall be worked out. Whether the United States shall actually acquire territorial possessions, shall set up captain-generalships and garrisons, whether they shall adopt the middle ground of protecting sovereignties nominally independent, or whether they shall content themselves with naval stations and diplomatic representatives as the basis for asserting their rights to the free commerce of the East, is a matter of detail. The discussion of the details may be of high importance to our political morality and our historical traditions, but it bears upon the economic side of the question only so far as a given political policy is necessary to safeguard and extend commercial interests. The writer is not an advocate of "imperialism" from sentiment, but does not fear the name if it means only that the United States shall assert their right to free markets in all the old countries which are being opened to the surplus resources of the capitalistic countries and thereby given the benefits of modern civilization. Whether this policy carries with it the direct government of groups of half-savage islands may be a subject for argument, but upon the economic side of the question there is but one choice — either to enter by some means upon the competition for the employment of American capital and enterprise in these countries, or to continue the needless duplication of existing means of production and communication, with the glut of unconsumed products, the convulsions followed by trade stagnation, and the steadily declining return upon investments which a negative policy will invoke.

The entry of the United States upon the

competition for the world's markets means some radical changes in their existing policy, but it means an enlarged share in the world's earnings and in the respect of other civilized states. The system of protection, whatever its original merits, will lose its importance when the producers of this country are able to compete in the markets of the world with the producers of all other countries. Great Britain has blazed the path of future economic achievement by declaring her willingness to open the gates of every country which she enters to the free competition of the world. The United States, if they would have her by their side, must follow the same course. The narrower policy pursued by France and Russia, of endeavoring to shut up their colonies to their own commerce, is only a repetition within a slightly extended wall of the old policy of building up trade, which should be reciprocal, by endeavoring to destroy the purchasing power of one's purchasers. Such a policy cannot offset the effects of congested capital, for it only intensifies within the protected wall the intensity of competition, and shuts up the producers to the barren contest against each other before the same body of consumers. Fictitious premiums set upon particular industries only make their last state worse than their first by drawing capital into such industries in excess of the requirements set by the natural laws of trade.

It is not even necessary to argue the question whether "trade follows the flag," or whether trade can be achieved without the prestige of political power. The present situation in China is such as to call for energetic political action on the part of all powers which desire to obtain new openings for their commerce. Russia, Germany, and France have seized stations and large tracts of territory in China, with a view to enforcing there their restrictive policy of shutting up the market to their own people. It is necessary, if the United States are to have an unimpaired share in the new trade of Asia, that they should protest against this policy of exclusion and seek to limit the area over which it is applied. Great Britain stands before the world, as she has done since the days of Huskisson and Peel, as the champion of free markets. The United States, if they are not to be excluded from Asia, must either sustain the policy of Great Britain, or they must follow the narrower policy of the continental countries in carving out a market of their own. Silent indifference to what is going on in Asia is not merely a question of political and naval prestige, or of territorial extension. It is a question whether the new markets which are being created there shall be opened to our commerce in any form under any conditions, and nothing but vigorous assertion of American interest in the subject will prevent the obstructions to the natural course of trade which will follow the division of Asia among the exclusionist powers of the European continent.

II

RUSSIA AS A WORLD POWER

WHEN Czar Nicholas II. recently determined to propose to Europe the modification of great armaments in the interest of the peace of the world, he acted from the far-sighted motives of public policy which have governed the economic measures of the Russian government for many years. The leaders of Russian political thought evidently reached the conclusion that Russia only needed relief from the heavy burden of taxation necessary for maintaining her great armies, to place her in the front rank among the industrial nations of the world. They have been for many years directing the steps of the empire in this direction, with a singleness of purpose and a continuity of policy which are rendered possible by the absolute form of the Russian government. To many Americans the Russian Empire still represents a half civilized state, peopled by the oppressed victims of a military tyranny in the older portions, and given up to barbarian hordes and army outposts in the provinces east of the Ural Mountains. Whatever warrant for this conception may have existed in the past, it is rapidly ceasing to be true. Russia is organizing the machinery of her economic system in a manner to make her the early and dangerous rival of the great industrial nations. M. de Witte, the Minister of Finance, furnishes the key of the present policy of the Russian government in the declarations of his last annual report to the Czar: —

> "The principal support of the economic and financial prosperity of Russia consists in the traditional policy, pacific and just, of her sovereigns. The principles bequeathed by the late Emperor Alexander III. and the sincere spirit of peace which animates your Majesty are guarantees that, in the future, as in the past, the foreign policy of Russia will be exempt from every aggressive disposition towards other states, with the view to the promotion of the well-being of our country, and that from this source our economic and financial system shall be menaced with no danger."

Whatever may be thought of the sincerity and truthfulness of this analysis of the foreign policy of Russia, the statement of the end to be sought — the care of the economic future of the country — is truthful and significant. M. Arthur Raffalovich, the accomplished financial agent of the Russian government in Paris, in his valuable annual volume on the financial development of the world, "Le Marché Financier en 1897–8," declares that the economic life of Russia has become the centre around which converges all the care of the government, the interest of the public, and the attention of foreign observers. "The country develops and concentrates its forces, and thus is able to accomplish the numerous reforms in other domains of Russian life, of which the need has long been felt."

This is a correct diagnosis of existing conditions in Russia. The whole energy of the state is being bent to the creation of a nation capable of competing in the field of manufactures, industry, commerce, and credit with the great Western nations and with the United States. Remarkable progress has been made towards this end. The present economic system of Russia is eminently paternal, but finds excuse in the comparative infancy of the nation in matters relating to commerce and credit. That this system has its evils, and leads the promoters of new projects "to consider the treasury of the state as an inexhaustible reservoir" for aiding their plans, is admitted by M. de Witte; but it seems for the moment to be the most efficient policy for equipping Russia with the means for entering upon the competition for political and commercial supremacy with the other industrial nations of the world.

The absence of parliamentary institutions, in spite of its latent evils, gives force, directness, and promptness to every measure decided upon for the development of the country. In a democratic state, it is necessary to convince the majority of the people before any great reform can be accomplished. In Russia, it is necessary to convince only the Czar and the Council of Ministers, which is made up of men trained for statecraft and undeterred from following their economic convictions by the exigencies of party politics. The leading statesmen of Russia are educated in the best schools of economics of France and Germany, they usually serve the state for many years when their services are efficient, and their combined experience and wisdom is applied to the important problems with which the government has had to deal in raising Russia from the condition of feudal times to a rank among civilized powers. There have been, within the limits of a little more than a generation, two striking illustrations in Russia of the difference between the power and efficiency of an absolute government in dealing with serious national problems, and a government where it is necessary to convince a majority of the people before action can be taken.

These two illustrations of the directness of the Russian government in proceeding toward an object, determined after consideration to be a desirable one, are of special interest to Americans, because they run parallel with two of their own great problems of the same period — the abolition of slavery and the restoration of order to the currency system. Russia liberated the serfs by a ukase of the Czar, at almost the very moment when the States of the American Union were plunging into civil war upon the same subject. She resumed specie payments upon the gold standard in 1897, after a series of well-considered steps which have made her currency system one of the most secure in the world. Each of these measures was carried out within a few years after the plans were matured, without bloodshed or popular upheaval, or paralysis of industry and credit.

While the final steps were being taken for the liberation of the serfs, upon a basis which compensated the owners and set the liberated class at once upon the footing of responsible property-owning subjects, the great Republic of the West was fighting a costly civil war, whose result was the liberation of the servile race, but without providing homes or a future for its members. A generation later, when the Russian Minister of Finance was calmly proceeding by successive steps to plant the credit of Russia upon an unassailable basis, the American Union was again torn with dissensions, banks were failing, industry was paralyzed, and Congress was sitting in extra session to undo the financial blunders to which the clamor of special interests and political cowardice had led a few years before.

The liberation of the serfs was conceived by Alexander II. soon after he succeeded to the power of Nicholas I. When the time came for action, in November, 1857, he issued a decree authorizing the Lithuanian nobles to form committees "to improve the condition of the serfs." He calmly assumed, in spite of some opposition on the part of the landholders, that they were favorable to reform, and followed up his policy in Lithuania by giving similar authority to the nobles in other provinces. A declaration in 1858 defined the principles of his plan, by which the peasants were to buy their houses and gardens, with land in addition sufficient for making a living, and were to be aided in the purchase by advances from the government to the landholders. A ukase of February 19, 1861, — the Russian proclamation of emancipation, — crowned the preliminary work and declared the abolition of serfdom.

The details of the financial operations by which this great reform was accomplished were set forth in a recent number of that invaluable mine of Russian statistics, the "Bulletin Russe de Statistique Financière et de Legislation." The indemnity allotted to landholders on account of the serfs from 1862 to 1891 reached the sum of 892,139,163 rubles ($450,000,000). Of this amount the government retained in various years 316,763,718 rubles to offset mortgage loans made to the landholders, and issued the remainder in 5 and $5\frac{1}{2}$ per cent. interest-bearing securities. The number of lots of land awarded to the serfs was 9,239,752, and the principal charged against them over a period of thirty years was 886,340,871 rubles. The aggregate amounts thus charged, including interest, from 1862 to 1891, were 1,040,167,863 rubles, and the amounts collected over the same period were 1,000,307,140 rubles ($520,000,000). The land was taken in many cases by associations of the serfs, which afforded a guarantee for payment, and left the question of individual distribution to local assemblies. This great work was not without incidental blunders and complaints, but it was accomplished without shock to the economic system, and has left the former serfs in no such position of irresponsible isolation as the emancipated race in the United States. The relative cost of the liberation of the serfs in Russia and the war for the preservation of the Union in the United States stands in the relation of about $500,000,000 in the case of Russia to $6,844,571,431 in the case of the United States.[1] Professor Seignobos, in his recent

[1] This is the computation of Professor Albert S. Bolles

"Political History of Contemporary Europe," after referring to the difficulties growing out of the small lots awarded to the serfs and the high valuation of the land in certain cases, says: —

"The emancipation of the serfs transformed Russian society. In giving to the mass of the population legal liberty and the administration of their local (communal) affairs, it has made of Russia a modern nation. It prepared her to deliver herself from habits of arbitrariness, servility, and laziness, produced by the long practice of servitude, and assured her the legal conditions of private enterprise and regular public administration. Economic progress was marked, after the death of Alexander II., by the increase in the area of cultivated lands, in the price of land, in the yield of the taxes, in the value of exports, and by the improvement in the peasant's manner of life."

The same energy and directness of action marked the measures taken to establish the gold standard which marked the plan for the liberation of the serfs. The accumulation of a gold reserve went on for many years under the management of far-sighted and highly educated ministers of finance, but the actual resumption of specie payments was delayed, first by the Crimean War and then by the

(*Financial History of the United States*, iii. 244), including $437,744,192 for army pensions to June 30, 1879.

war with Turkey in 1877. When the gold reserve of the Treasury and the Imperial Bank had risen on January 1, 1895, to about $500,000,000, M. de Witte, the Minister of Finance, laid before the Czar a carefully matured plan for giving a fixed value to the circulating paper money and gradually reaching the free interchange of gold and paper at the bank. From the beginning of 1895 to the beginning of 1897, a period of two years, successive decrees were issued, which gradually accomplished all that the ministry had planned, and placed the Russian Empire, without disturbance to vested rights or business interests, among the gold standard nations of the world.

A national three per cent. gold loan was issued for reimbursing to the Imperial Bank a part of its advances to the Treasury; gold contracts were authorized; special gold accounts were received at the bank and gold check-books issued; gold certificates were issued and made legal tender for public dues; 693,000,000 rubles ($350,000,000) in gold was paid out during 1896 by the Treasury and the bank; a fixed exchange value was given to the paper ruble; and gold coins were provided for at the new rate of exchange. Gold is now freely paid for notes at the bank, and the gradual contraction of the note circulation, with the increase of the gold funds to $600,000,000, has increased the gold above the amount of the outstanding paper and given the notes of the Bank of Russia the character of gold certificates. The effect of these measures was discussed intelligently by the leading financial journals and aroused some differences of opinion, but there was no attempt to inflame the prejudice of the masses against the policy of the government; there were no windy demagogues stumping the provinces declaring that "the gold standard is a conspiracy against the human race." Scant attention would have been given to such orators by the absolute government of Russia, but intelligent discussion by responsible economic students was cordially welcomed and carefully weighed in the councils of the Czar.

The part which Russia has been playing since the early eighties as a grain-producing country is well known on the world's exchanges, and will be passed over here for a few references to her growth in more highly organized industries. It is worth noting, in passing, that in the production of petroleum, Russia has become within a few years a serious competitor of the United States. The production of 1881 was 663,001 metric tons against a production in the United States of 4,612,600 such tons, the part of the United States in the production of the two countries being 874 in 1000. The production of Russia increased to 3,183,418 tons in 1888, while that of the United States remained substantially unchanged. Both countries have advanced with rapid strides during the succeeding ten years, but Russia is now practically abreast of this country in the production of the world's supply. The latest complete Russian figures were those of 1895, when the production of the United States was 8,835,181 metric tons and of Russia 7,056,537 tons; but the single district of Baku in 1896 and 1897 almost equaled the entire Russian product of 1895 and greatly exceeded that of 1894.

The most striking evidence of the entry of Russia into the list of competing capitalistic countries is afforded by the incorporation of stock companies in recent years. A recent number of the "Bulletin Russe de Statistique" brought the list of mining, metal-working, naphtha, and salt companies down to June 14, 1898. The whole number of such corporations constituted under Russian laws was 205, with an aggregate capital of a little more than 500,000,000 rubles ($260,000,000). Of this number 125 companies have been constituted since January 1, 1895, and these include nearly all of the companies with large capitals, ranging from 18,000,000 rubles downward. This is only a part of the list of Russian stock companies. Banking and credit societies are in operation to the number of 548, with a subscribed capital of 285,211,356 rubles, exclusive of the Imperial Bank and its many branches. There are 293 corporations devoted to commerce and public works, life insurance, navigation, gas, and electricity, with a subscribed capital of 176,124,144 rubles. There are also 536 industrial corporations, with a capital of 596,550,501 rubles. The 1377 corporations, with an aggregate capital of 1,058,886,301 rubles ($550,000,000), include all those paying the tax of five per cent. upon net profits, and the net profits reported averaged 13.06

per cent., running as high as 16.9 per cent. in the case of the discount banks, 36.8 per cent. in the case of the food societies, and to even higher figures in the case of certain special industries.

A statement of all the business enterprises subject to the patent tax (or business license) in 1895 shows transactions amounting to 8,739,087,700 rubles ($4,500,000,000) for wholesale enterprises, with profits of 316,-547,450 rubles ($160,000,000), and transactions of 955,051,900 rubles ($490,000,000) for retail enterprises subject to the tax, with profits of 102,212,680 rubles ($53,000,000). The figures of the total transactions or receipts of various companies include about $1,700,000,000 on account of the money paid into banks in the course of current transactions, but even if this amount is deducted, a total industrial activity, important enough to be subject to tax, amounting to $3,250,-000,000, represents no small volume of business for a country whose economic development is so recent as that of Russia. All these figures, moreover, are taken from the tax returns for 1895. The growth of economic activity since that time has enormously increased the number of corporations, the volume of transactions, and the collections on account of the government. The revenue collected from the patent and additional taxes increased from 28,934,339 rubles ($15,000,000) in 1887 to 42,760,721 rubles in 1895 and 48,167,400 rubles in 1898.

The development of Russia as a manufacturing and capitalistic country is raising there the same industrial questions which have arisen in Great Britain, France, Belgium, Germany, and the United States. The Russian labor laws did not regulate until recently any work except that of children, youths, and women, and the relation between the laborer and his employer. A step in the path of other industrial countries was taken by the law of June 2, 1897, which fixed definite hours of labor for adult males. The law was granted as much to meet the wishes of large manufacturers, in order to meet the competition of establishments having an excessively long day, as in response to the demands of the laboring men themselves. The working day is still long, but the system of limitation which has been put in operation is likely to be continued, with the increased productive power of the laborer and the increase of his earnings, until the Russian factory hand stands upon a level with his fellow in Western Europe and America. The law of June 2 extended the regulations regarding the inspection of labor and contracts with laborers to the whole of European Russia and Poland. The number of inspectors of labor was increased from 151 to 171, and the labor laws were extended to all establishments which employ sixteen or more skilled laborers.

Technical education is finding a large place in the policy of the Russian government. There were twelve higher technical schools in the country in 1896, containing 5916 pupils. Schools of commerce were opened in 1897 under a law of April 15, 1896, at Kiew, Odessa, Varsovia, Moscow, Kharkow, Nijni-Novgorod, St. Petersburg, and Lodz. A school of navigation has just been opened at Odessa, which is recommended by the United States consul for imitation in this country. Professional primary schools were opened in many other towns, and agricultural schools and schools of horticulture in the farming provinces of both European Russia and Siberia. Projects of law were recently under consideration by the Department of Finance for the revision of existing legislation on stock companies, the creation of corporations for popular readings and libraries, a new code for commercial paper, the regulation of weights and measures, the reduction of duties upon agricultural machinery and manure, and a new classification of the *octroi* charges in cities. The tariff rates on agricultural machinery were reduced in 1893 and 1894, and the value of the imports of such articles rose from 2,644,230 rubles in 1888 to 5,286,954 rubles in 1896.

One of the best tests of the economic progress of a nation is the extent and flexibility of its system of credit. The deposit and check system has not attained the development in Russia which it has attained in some other commercial countries, but is gaining ground at a remarkable rate. The discounts at the Imperial Bank were 132,578,530 rubles on October 23, 1898, exclusive of the accounts at the branches,[1] and the deposit

[1] The amount on January 1, 1900, was 226,803,930 rubles, but a part of this increase was probably due to the efforts of the bank to support credit after the crisis of the preceding autumn, and does not represent a normal growth.

accounts included 61,918,009 rubles payable on demand to individuals and 84,531,307 rubles to the account of other bankers, credit societies, and industrial and commercial corporations. Private commercial banks are rapidly obtaining a footing in Russia. There were forty such institutions in 1897, of which nine were at St. Petersburg, with a capital and surplus of 119,000,000 rubles; four at Moscow, with a capital of 36,300,000 rubles; and twenty-seven in the provinces, with capital and surplus of 86,300,000 rubles. The deposits in these forty banks on October 10, 1897, were 476,800,000 rubles ($240,000,000), an increase of 86,700,000 rubles within a year. The deposits at St. Petersburg amounted to 219,000,000 rubles, and at Moscow to 117,600,000 rubles.

The statutes of the Bank of Russia were subjected to a complete revision in 1894, and the new statutes, promulgated on June 24, 1894, declared the purpose of the bank to be "to facilitate, by means of credit for short terms, the movement of commerce, and to promote the success of national industry and agricultural production." Besides the usual provisions for loans upon commercial paper, the bank was authorized within carefully guarded limits to make advances on agricultural products and industrial material. The maximum loan for industrial enterprises is 500,000 rubles, and for a retail merchant 600 rubles. The maximum term for loans for material is three years, but periodical payments are required when the term exceeds six months. The bank is authorized to accept, as security for loans to small farmers, peasants, and mechanics, the guarantee of the provincial assemblies, mutual credit societies, and individuals chosen from among the inhabitants of the community who are satisfactory to the bank. The government made advances to the peasants of some 90,000,000 rubles during the famine of 1892 and the customs war with Germany in 1893, which were repaid only in installments over a considerable period of time.

Popular banks for assisting peasants and mechanics of small means are rapidly spreading over Russia. The beginning of 1897 found 720 of these associations in operation, of which the 608 making complete returns counted 218,100 members, with deposits of 9,200,000 rubles. A congress was held at

Moscow in March, 1898, for the study of questions relating to the extension of small credits, and to consider a plan for a central bank for supporting the rural banks, as in Germany and Austria. The growth of the Russian savings deposits has been phenomenal in recent years. The balances due depositors were only 9,054,648 rubles ($4,600,000) in 1880. This rose in 1890 to 147,042,901 rubles, and in 1895 to 377,165,352 rubles. The latest available report, giving the deposits at the end of August, 1898, shows balances of 508,512,000 rubles ($260,000,000) distributed among 2,675,536 separate accounts.[1] An analysis of the accounts was published in 1898, which showed that on January 1, 1897, the farming population had on deposit 66,437,000 rubles; mechanics in the cities, 33,288,000 rubles; factory employees, 12,076,000 rubles; merchants, 34,588,000 rubles; and domestics, 29,829,000 rubles. An interesting indication of the improvement in the conditions of living, such as was noted in England earlier in the century, is the increased consumption of sugar. The taxes

[1] The report for February 1, 1900, showed deposits of 614,376,000 rubles ($320,000,000), and 3,172,858 accounts.

paid upon this product were only 23,161,725 rubles in 1888; they were 58,561,800 rubles in 1898.

The Russian railway system is also attaining a development which is putting the country abreast of the great transportation systems of the world. A comparison of the mileage in 1895 showed Russia, not including Finland and Siberia, in the possession of 36,585 kilometres of line, while France had 36,337 kilometres. The figures on January 1, 1898, gave Russia, including Siberia, 40,300 kilometres. With the addition of the trans-Siberian line and the construction of the past few years, Russia is ahead of France in actual mileage, although still below her in length of line *per capita*. Railway earnings have steadily increased with the development of commerce and the extension of connecting lines. The gross earnings in 1881 were only 199,979,356 rubles ($103,000,000), and the net earnings 55,538,549 rubles ($28,000,000). The gross earnings of 1897 were 447,359,975 rubles, and the net earnings were 181,481,219 rubles ($94,000,000).

These figures do not approach those of the United States, where the gross earnings in 1896 were $1,125,632,025 upon 180,891 miles of operated lines, and the net earnings were $332,333,756; but American railroad men may well regard with envy the percentage of net earnings in Russia, which is nearly 45 per cent. of gross income, in comparison with the less than 30 per cent. of such earnings on American lines. The number of persons employed on the Russian lines in 1895 was 343,996, and their combined earnings were 109,795,743 rubles ($55,000,000). M. Raffalovich declares that the existing lines do not meet the constantly growing needs of Russian commerce. The transportation of merchandise over the lines of the west has especially increased since the opening of the trans-Siberian. The four existing ports are hardly capable of handling the commerce of the Baltic, and it has frequently happened that grain transports have been stopped on the way to these ports because proper provision could not be made for discharging and receiving their cargoes.

The most important achievement of Russian railway engineering — the result at the same time of enlightened political foresight — is the trans-Siberian railway. This long thread of steel, connecting European Russia with the Pacific, was a dream of Russian statesmen as far back as 1850. It was not until the opening of the Ural line in 1880, which joined Perm, in European Russia, with Tiumen, on the Tobol, which flows into the Irtish, that a long practical step was taken towards binding the empire together by a single railway system. Several parts of the line remain to be completed in Russian territory, but the most important uncompleted part is the Eastern Chinese railway, across the northern province of China. M. Pierre Leroy-Beaulieu, who recently traversed the line, and describes his observations in the "Revue des Deux Mondes" for August 15, 1898, expresses the opinion that it will not be completed for ten years. The contract has already been signed, however, for obtaining the money from the Russo-Chinese Bank, and the control of the road, although under a Chinese president, is substantially under the Russian Minister of Finance.

The entire line, from the foot of the Ural to Vladivostock, on the Pacific Ocean, will have a length of 6613 kilometres, or about 4200 miles. It will be by far the shortest route from Europe to the Orient. The time from London to Hongkong is now twenty-five days by the Suez Canal and thirty-three days by way of the Canadian Pacific Railway. It will be reduced to twenty days by the trans-Siberian. The advantage in the case of other European places and Asiatic ports farther north will be much greater. The trip from Paris to Pekin can be made in sixteen days, where it now requires thirty-four days from France or England to Yokohama by the Suez Canal and twenty-five days by way of Canada. The passenger charges, moreover, are computed by M. Leroy-Beaulieu, including sleeping-cars and meals, at about 800 francs ($160) from Paris to northern China, as compared with charges of 1800 francs ($360) by the present steamer routes. The charges will be less favorable upon bulky freight from Western Europe, but for the interior of Russia the opening of the railway means that the resources of the East are at her disposal, and that she can deliver in the East her own products at a great advantage over her Western rivals.

Business men throughout Europe will benefit by the mail service over the new railway, which will deliver letters in sixteen or eighteen days, in place of the month or five weeks now required. But the Russian merchants will enjoy the advantage of quicker communication and nearness to their new markets. The opening of new routes of communication has often involved the rise and fall of nations. It would not be contrary to historical precedents if, in the course of years, the development of the great trans-continental route which binds European Russia to Siberia should shift the centres of trade in the East, destroy the importance of many existing ports in China, and create new commercial centres in the heart of Asia, around which will gather the civilization of coming generations.

It is not surprising that Russian statesmen, with the vista of the economic empire of the future within their grasp, hampered by no necessity for pandering to the clamor of the moment in order to keep themselves in office, should have determined that Russia would gain enormously in the race with other industrial nations by devoting her whole energies to economic development. Hence the proposition of the Czar, that the world lay aside its arms, and give its people an opportunity to devote themselves to industrial pursuits, looks directly to the future dominance of Russia in the commerce and finance of the world. It would be useless for Russia to attempt to fight such a power as Great Britain in the East until the completion of the trans-Siberian railway. She has accomplished wonderful results by the firmness and audacity of her diplomacy in China. When the railway is completed, with the economic development which will come in another period of ten years, she will be able to cope on land, if not on the ocean, with any force which can be brought against her. She will enjoy the advantage of occupying the inner line, from which she can strike at her enemies on the European or Asiatic flank with the force and directness of Napoleon when he was able to carry out his favorite policy of separating and conquering hostile armies.

Ten years of such economic development as Russia has witnessed in the ten years just passed will make her enormously stronger than she is to-day; thirty years will make her almost irresistible. With a government controlled by the single purpose of promoting national advancement, with the best economic knowledge of all peoples at her command, with almost unlimited natural resources, and with an equipment of producing plant and saved capital sufficient to permit constantly accelerating progress, Russia promises in another generation to be the great competitor of the Anglo-Saxon race for the commercial and military supremacy of the world.

III

THE STRUGGLE FOR COMMERCIAL EMPIRE

The recent appearance of the Russian government as a possible borrower in the New York money market is a trifling financial incident in itself; but it is an indication of the change which has come over the economic condition of the world within the last few years. It shows that the United States are approaching the position of a creditor nation, able to lend their surplus capital to debtor nations; and it affords a hint of the earnest effort which Russia is making to develop her internal economic life in order to put herself abreast of other industrial countries.

The civilized nations of the world are entering a contest for financial and commercial supremacy upon a grander scale than any in the past, and upon a field which is being rapidly extended over the decadent and undeveloped nations. The contests for commercial supremacy down to the beginning of the present century were mainly between hand-workers, in which even the most successful nation did not increase by a large percentage its direct productive power, as has been the case within the present century by the application of steam and electricity to nearly all forms of production and transportation. The beginning of the nineteenth century witnessed the first really great savings of capital over and above the demands of current consumption. The progress of the century witnessed the gradual equipment of a few highly civilized nations with the machinery of production and exchange. This process of equipment was substantially completed in 1873, with which year the long period of depression set in which some have ascribed, by a natural error, to changes in the monetary standard. The fact that this change in regard to the standard monetary metal — whatever the academic merits of the controversy between bimetallism and the single standard — was only an incident in modern economic development is now gradually dawning upon thoughtful minds, and revealing the true cause of existing conditions, the overequipment of the great industrial nations with the machinery of production and with surplus capital, and the need for new markets and new fields of investment. Society, in the long run, instinctively acts along the lines of natural development; and even before economists discerned clearly the real cause of the long period of depression, the European nations were reaching out their commerce and political power in order to secure new outlets for their overproduction of finished goods and for their great accumulations of capital. In these respects, the United States have been gradually attaining the condition of the industrial nations of Europe. Our turn has come to participate in the struggle for foreign markets; and apparently as the result of an accident in Havana Harbor, the path of destiny has been suddenly opened for us in the East.

Accidents are only the ripening of opportunity. It has been by no series of accidents, not even by the thirst for military grandeur apart from its economic results, that the great civilized states have been expanding their spheres of influence in all quarters of the world. It was an economic necessity which precipitated the British occupation of Egypt; and it was the pressure of surplus capital which led to the opening up of "the Dark Continent," and has made its map a checker-board of English, French, German, Belgian, Italian, and Portuguese dependencies. The threatened partition of China — already well under way by Russia, France, Germany, and Great Britain — is another phase of the same great movement; and the occupation of Cuba and the Philippines by the United States only marks the entry of the latter into the contest for financial and commercial supremacy. Great Britain has always had her anti-imperialists; and the French fleet in 1882 withdrew from before Alexandria, and left the British to save Egypt to civilization. But the inexorable progress of economic tendencies has made expansion the inevitable policy of states which would survive in the future. Mr. Benjamin Kidd has admirably expressed the situation in his recent monograph, "The Control of the Tropics:" —

"It is probably true, however strange it may appear to say so, that, at the present day, the far-reaching effects of the part which the English-speaking peoples are probably destined to play in the future are not so much thought of, or even so clearly perceived, either in England or in America, as they are by some of the more far-seeing minds in France and Germany. It is to this cause that we may trace a very pronounced tendency of which the effects have been very distinctly felt in England of late years. More than one of these thinkers, perceiving the vast future consequences of that expansion of the English-speaking peoples, towards which the entire drift of policy and events amongst these peoples for the last two hundred years has tended, has become convinced also that it is necessary that his own nation should embark, before it is too late, in a policy of expansion. More clearly than either in England or in America is it perceived that, as the result of existing developments, the world outside of Europe tends in the future to be controlled in the main by only two sets of forces, those which proceed from the peoples who speak English, and those which proceed from the peoples who speak Russian. The temperate regions, it is seen, have already been occupied. But there remain the tropics."

One of the most striking phenomena of the new economic conditions is the rapidity with which capitalization proceeds, when once a country has entered, to any considerable extent, upon the career of machine production. This has been illustrated in a remarkable manner by the history of Germany and Russia during the last twenty-five years. In

1870 Germany was a comparatively poor country. It was not merely the direct transfer of $1,000,000,000 in credits from France, by way of a war indemnity, which enriched her, but the stimulus which this event gave to her industrial development. Speculation ran riot for a time, as in most countries which have just entered upon an industrial career; but the result has been an enormous manufacturing development at home, and the accumulation of capital which has permitted large investments abroad. The estimated wealth of Germany in negotiable securities in 1895 was $18,000,000,000; and she ranked second among European nations. The number of banks reporting in 1883 to the imperial government was 119, with a capital of 1,248,700,000 marks, and reserves of 174,400,000 marks; or a total equaling, say, $340,000,000. The number reporting in 1897 had increased, in spite of numerous consolidations, to 150, with a capital of 2,163,500,000 marks, and reserves of 461,200,000 marks; making a total equivalent to about $630,000,000. The capital of the 11 large Berlin banks, exclusive of the Imperial Bank, increased from 586,000,000 marks, at the close of 1896, to 844,000,000 marks ($200,000,000) in 1898.

These German banks, with the large capital at their command derived from the proceeds of German industry during the last twenty-five years, are reaching out in all directions at home, and as the competitors of British and French capital abroad. At home, large amounts are being absorbed for lighting-plants, and sewage and water systems. Town and provincial loans, which amounted in 1894 to $25,000,000, rose in 1897 to $47,000,000, and in the first half of 1898 to $26,000,000. New industrial joint stock companies, whose shares were issued during 1894 to the amount of only $23,000,000, increased their issues in 1895 to $58,000,000; in 1897 to $70,000,000; and for the first half of 1898 to $65,000,000. It is estimated that in Germany alone the electrical industry, including city and suburban railways, absorbs about $75,000,000 of German capital annually, and that about $50,000,000 is invested annually in electrical undertakings in foreign countries. The year 1897 witnessed the construction of 452 miles of electric lines in Germany,

France, Austria, Italy, and England, of which Germany built more than two thirds.

German capital seeking investment has been so plentiful that it was tempted by the low prices of Spanish securities during the war with the United States; and from July to the autumn there was an increase in such securities held in Germany from 50,000,000 pesetas to 150,000,000 pesetas ($29,000,000). The amount of Russian loans held in Germany is computed at $370,000,000. German enterprise and German capital are confronting British and French investors in banks and industrial enterprises in Latin America, in Africa, and in Asia. The December number of the London "Bankers' Magazine," in a review of the financial history of 1898, declared: —

"Among the poorer countries, or the countries in which, though capital may have existed, it was not in a form available for immediate use, like the less settled parts of Europe and Asia Minor and the further East, the aid of English capital usually used to be invoked. But we now find things managed differently; other sources are open to those who engage in such undertakings, and great railways are established through the interposition of German banks. Some ten years since, the Deutsche Bank took over the Société du Chemin de Fer Ottoman d'Anatolie, and commenced the Anatolian railways. Since then it has constructed the supplementary Anatolian line from Eskishehr to Konia. Meanwhile it constructed in European Turkey, in Macedonia, the line Saloniki-Monastia. The same bank has likewise obtained a great many concessions for the further development of the Anatolian system of railways."

The development of Russia has been, in some respects, even more remarkable than that of Germany. In 1895 she was reported as possessing only $5,000,000,000 in negotiable securities; but the issues of the shares of stock companies in Russia amounted in 1895 to 129,363,000 rubles, in 1896 to 232,640,000 rubles, in 1897 to 239,424,000 rubles, and in 1898 to 256,237,000 rubles. New textile mills, paper mills, mortgage banks, and discount banks are being established almost every week; and their mere enumeration fills pages of nearly every number of the Russian statistical publication, the "Bulletin Russe de Statistique." Russian capital united with French capital in 1895 to create the Russo-Chinese Bank, which is now one of the most important instruments of Russian financial and political influence in China. Russia is still a large debtor nation, but is employing her own and borrowed capital in the development of her internal resources in the connection of European Russia with her possessions in the East, and in carrying out a policy intended to make her the potent rival of the great industrial nations.

Great Britain, the first of the great capitalist nations of modern times, which, at the beginning of the century, was already seeking investments in South America, and sending British money to her colonial possessions in India, has witnessed a peculiar development within the last few years. Her control of the banking business of the world and the freedom of commercial exchanges, which brought the products of the nations to London and Liverpool for distribution by British ships and British merchants to other quarters of the earth, have long enabled her to live, to a large extent, upon her investments. This has been shown by the great excess of her imports over her exports of merchandise. This "unfavorable balance of trade," in the old mercantilist jargon, is the evidence of her command over the capital and resources of the world, by which interest on her great loans is paid in commodities instead of in gold. The control of the exchanges alone, by means of the colonial banks with London offices, and the banks organized with British capital in foreign countries, has been an immense source of profit. These banks, numbering twenty-three foreign joint stock companies with London offices, and twenty-nine colonial banks with their head offices in London, possessed at the beginning of 1898 combined capital and reserves of £69,-000,000 and deposits of £210,000,000. A dividend of only four per cent. upon the capital of this investment would pay more than $13,000,000 per year; and much larger dividends have been paid by many institutions, such as the Hongkong and Shanghai Banking Corporation, the London and River Plate Bank, with its large holdings of the shares of tributary banks, and other instruments of British financial power.

The magnitude of British investments abroad has greatly increased the excess of imports of merchandise over exports within the last few years. For the five years ending with 1890 the average annual excess was $453,533,467; the average for the five years ending with 1895 rose to $669,255,-679; while the excess for the year 1898 approximated $1,000,000,000. This condition of things has excited some alarm among certain persons in Great Britain, who regard it as evidence of the decline of British industry. This is not the occasion for discussing the merits of this question; but the mere decline of certain manufactures and the increase in the excess of imports are not in themselves an indication of anything more than the transfer of capital to more productive enterprises in foreign countries. Great Britain, according to recent estimates, has capital invested abroad to the amount of £2,000,000,000, or nearly $10,000,000,000. The interest upon this sum, at 4½ per cent., would bring her an annual revenue of $450,-000,000; and she derives a like amount from the passenger and freight earnings of her merchant marine. So far as these foreign investments are safe and well chosen, British capitalists, in sending their capital abroad, are only following the natural law of unhampered trade, — that capital is transferred to the industries affording the greatest profits. The result is much more beneficial to British interests than if the increasing savings of the country were kept at home to bid against each other in the stock market. Such a competition, in a country already equipped with the tools of production and exchange, results in the needless duplication of existing plant, and in the rise of first-class securities to such a price that they cease to afford an adequate return upon the capital invested.

The necessity of sending capital abroad to obtain profitable returns is the salient economic lesson of the closing days of the nineteenth century. In recent years interest and discount rates have been declining, as the result of the excess of loanable capital beyond the effective demand of European markets, and of the diminishing return paid by first-class investments at home. The facts under this head — indicating that first-class securities in Great Britain, France, and Germany were paying only 2½ per cent., and that French industry was, to some extent, feeding upon itself without increasing the actual return upon invested capital — have already been pointed out.

The opponents of colonial expansion often discuss the question of foreign markets as though the only question were the absorption of finished goods. This is in reality the less important side of the problem. The real opportunity afforded by colonial possessions is for the development of the new countries by fixed investments, whose slow completion is the only present means of absorbing saved capital without its waste by company promoters upon visionary projects. Whether trade invariably follows the flag or not, the real question of the benefits of Australia, India, Canada, and Egypt to Great Britain, and of Algeria, Tunis, and Madagascar to France, relates to the fields which have been and will be opened there for the profitable investment of capital, and not merely to the quantity of finished goods laid down annually in the export trade. The development of a new country by means of railways, roads, and docks is the forerunner of higher civilization, better wages, enlarged wants, and increased consumption. The benefits of this larger market for goods usually fall to the country which provides the capital for the primary development, especially if it is that country also which, by its political control, affords the guarantees of security and order.

The energy with which the settled countries of Europe are seeking these opportunities for the investment of their capital has only recently begun to attract the attention of the American people. We have been absorbed for many years in the development of our industries at home, and have only recently begun to feel the effects of diminished discount and interest rates and the pressure of surplus capital upon the means for its absorption. How extensively the leading countries of Europe have been absorbing territory in Africa and Asia is indicated by a recent report of the United States commercial agent at Weimar regarding the colonial possessions of European states. He shows that, outside the mother country, Great Britain holds 16,662,073 square miles of territory, with a population of 322,000,000; France, 2,505,000 miles, with a population of nearly 50,000,000; Germany, 1,615,577 miles, with a population of 7,450,000; Holland, 783,000 miles, with a population of 34,210,000; and Portugal, 809,914 miles, with a population of 10,215,000.

The mere occupation of these territories is only the beginning of the process of development upon which the occupying countries have entered. The entire face of the world, in relation to its centres of production and routes of trade, is likely to be transformed within the next two generations. As the Mediterranean lost its importance when ocean-going vessels passed outside the Pillars of Hercules, and America and India became the objective points of European commerce, so the evolution of the next half century is likely to develop new trade centres in Asia and Africa. This shifting of the axis of commerce will be strongly affected by the great railway routes which are in process of completion or in contemplation. Within a few years Russia will complete the trans-Siberian railway, which will shorten the journey from Paris to the Pacific by many days, and will make Russia much closer to Japan and China, by way of Siberia, than England and France can ever be by the ocean. A recent consular report announced that a branch of the South Siberian Railroad, leading to the borders of Afghanistan, was opened for business, and that the first trip was made on November 20, 1898. This road, it is declared, "is the key to Afghanistan, the borders of Persia, and, above all, the capital city of Herat and the great valley of Heri-Rud."

Within a short time the French government will probably take up the construction of the trans-Saharian road, which will bind her flourishing provinces of Algiers and Tunis to Timbuctoo and the Soudan. It is nearly a quarter of a century since the trans-Saharian was first broached, and several years since the first link was planned by the Ministry of Public Works. Actual work has not yet been begun; but M. Paul Leroy-Beaulieu, the eminent French economist, seized upon the withdrawal of the French from Fashoda to point out repeatedly, in the journals for which he writes, that the trans-Saharian is essential to French domination in Africa, and that under its operation France would not only be in a position to transfer a large army in a fortnight from Algiers to the heart of Africa and to threaten British control of the Soudan, but would also open a new world to trade. The heart of Africa, which Stanley penetrated through so many dangers, is likely to become in a few years an easy journey of a few days, in a Pullman sleeper, from French civilization on the northern coast.

The opening of these railways means the development of great areas of country which have not heretofore been factors in Western civilization. They will not at the outset provide large crops, large supplies of finished goods, or large bodies of consumers; but every new step in development will add to the degree of civilization of the people, and will make them at once larger producers and larger consumers. It will be in no way surprising if a great emporium of trade develops in Central Asia, once the prolific nursery of the Tartar hordes which swept in successive waves across Europe. Central Africa is less favorably situated, from a climatic point of view, for the creation of a commercial centre inhabited by Europeans; but Northern Africa, under French domination, may resume the place it held in the time of Hamilcar and Hannibal, if the restrictive policy of France gives place to an invitation to all nations to share in her trade. The great Sahara Desert is already being traversed by French engineers, and a letter in "l'Economiste Français" of November 19, 1898, declares that a single plateau alone around Air, or Asben, possesses an area equal to a quarter of that of France, of which a large portion is susceptible of cultivation.

While this reaching out for the markets of the world is going on, the United States cannot afford to adhere to the policy of isolation. The domestic market for finished goods has long since been more than supplied; and it is one of the encouraging symptoms of the new order of things that American manufactured goods are finding new markets abroad. The exports of American manufactures, which as recently as 1888 were only $130,300,087, were $253,681,541 in 1896, $279,652,721 in 1897, and reached $307,924,994 in 1898. The exports of manufactures from the United States in the latter year surpassed the imports of manufactures for the first time. It is obvious that the United States are rapidly approaching the condition of Great Britain, France, Germany, and Belgium, where they will be compelled to seek free markets and opportunities for investment in the undeveloped countries, if they are not to be crowded to the wall by the efforts of the other great civilized powers. The efficiency of machine production, combined with the saving of capital for investment, which restricts the consumption of finished goods, is such that no advanced industrial nation will hereafter find a sufficient market at home for its products, or will derive any essential benefit from stimulating an excess of production in particular directions by artificial means. This process may have its value while the country is not self-sufficing in its production of machine-made goods; but it is without avail when it enters upon the competition for commerce abroad.

The United States are rapidly becoming self-sufficing in respect to their supplies of available capital, as well as in the volume of their machine production. A wonderful change has come over their financial and economic conditions within the last six years. It is only within that time that bad financial legislation drove gold abroad, paralyzed industry, and brought American securities back upon the New York market by millions in 1893. The crisis was passed without abandoning the monetary standard of other civilized nations; and it may be a question whether the ultimate results did not contribute, at a high cost, to hasten the financial independence which may make New York in the future a competitor of London for the control of the world's money markets.

Financial independence is a desirable thing when it can be safely attained. It is not desirable when it is obtained by the expulsion of foreign capital which might be employed at a profit over and above the cost of its rental. The events of 1893 and the three following years subjected the American people to severe losses, which were largely due to the withdrawal of foreign capital through distrust of our financial policy. In the three fiscal years ending with June 30, 1896, the United States exported $415,611,064 more merchandise than was imported, and exported also $235,000,000 more of the precious metals. This was an excess of more than $200,000,000 over the amount required for the payment of freights to foreign vessels and interest due abroad. This loss was largely covered by the return of American securities to this country, in addition to the strain put upon our resources by the unwonted experience of paying interest in full on foreign loans, instead of getting the benefit of their constant reinvestment here.

The four years which followed the summer

of 1896 showed the same great excess of American exports over imports which marked the previous three years, but under entirely different conditions. The United States now appears to be buying back American securities held abroad, not, as was the case in 1893 and 1894, at the cost of bankrupt railways and paralyzed industry, but because she chooses to do it out of her abundant surplus. The year 1898 witnessed a constantly expanding volume of commerce at home, which afforded the means for large purchases of foreign goods. Such purchases have not been taking place; and the imports for 1898 were less than those of any preceding year since 1885. In the mean time there has been a turn of the tide of gold toward this country, which affords the best evidence that, if American securities are being purchased in foreign markets, it is no longer because the foreigner is unloading them at any sacrifice, in order to recover his money, but because the American purchaser has the means to pay a good price. These two and a half years have created an apparent balance of another sum of $200,000,000 in favor of the United States, after making liberal deduction for freights to foreign vessels, interest owed abroad, and expenditures by tourists. The United States, therefore, so far as these figures have definite value, is $400,000,000 nearer to financial independence than she was five years ago. It was estimated at that time that $2,000,000,000 of foreign capital was invested in this country. This has since been materially reduced; and the capital which remains is likely to be left permanently at the disposition of American financiers.

The rapidity with which New York has gained upon the other great money centres of the world within the last few years is indicated by the increase of her banking business. The year 1898 witnessed larger operations through the clearing-house than any previous year since the creation of the Stock Exchange Clearing-House; and the loans of the banks at the beginning of December nearly doubled those of 1886. All the leading banks of the city, including both the national banks and the state banks which do business through the clearing-house, had loans on March 4, 1899, amounting to $780,607,700, and deposits amounting to $914,810,300. The corresponding figures for March

16, 1889, just ten years ago, showed loans of $420,406,000, and deposits of $442,684,-900.

Striking confirmation of the declaration of Mr. Kidd — that the far-reaching effects of the part to be played by the English-speaking peoples in the world's future battle for commercial empire are more generally and clearly perceived on the European Continent than at home — comes from European economic students. "L'Economiste Européen," one of the most accurate of the French financial journals, contains in its issue of December 23, 1898, an article which emphasizes in forcible language the fact that the United States are attaining commercial independence and are threatening the European nations in all their markets. "The United States of America and the Disunited States of Europe" is the warning title with which Professor Marcel Dubois, of the University of Paris, heads his article. In the gradual growth of the self-sufficiency of the United States to supply her own markets he finds the controlling reason which has led France, Germany, Italy, and Belgium to seek openings in Africa. Even the hope of a compensation in China for lost markets in America M. Dubois sees threatened by the young giant of the West, whose growth he thus describes: —

"In spite of respectful and courteous formalities which are exchanged across the Atlantic, the actual state of the relations between Europe and America reveals to us the progress of the economic emancipation of a world which begins to count a self-sufficing population, possessing, by means of its growing numbers and its industrial progress, a less and less quantity of natural products for exportation and receiving already a diminished number of immigrants. Hence the spectacle of a decreasing export trade on the part of the old industrial peoples of Europe, who encounter a sharp competition on the other side of the Atlantic, and yet, in spite of the diminished profits upon the sale of their products, are some of them unable to dispense with the food supplies of the New World. It is a true state of crisis, an armed peace."

It is little wonder that the French professor, with this drama of the future in his vision, closes by a warning to the Old World — "disunited, divided, absorbed in quarrels, stimulated by the ardor of historic traditions rather than by consciousness of real interest" — to unite "against the monopolists of the ocean and of colonial commerce, whether they be of one nation or of two."

The United States, therefore, with New

York as their chief city, stand at the close of the nineteenth century upon the threshold of the commercial and financial empire of the world. They are equipped, by the confession of their rivals, with a strength which fits them to contend for financial supremacy with the great European money centres, provided they adopt policies which will permit their people to enter unfettered upon the race.

The United States should adopt a monetary system which will give certainty to exchanges, and a banking system which will give them elasticity. The adoption of the gold standard by Great Britain in 1818 gave the assurance to every buyer and acceptor of a bill of exchange that he would receive a fixed weight of gold in London. There was no loss of exchange to be reckoned with, as in the case of an alternating standard; so that the rates of exchange could be reduced to the actual cost of transferring money and capital. Mr. Walter Bagehot well states the advantage which London enjoyed over Paris in this respect, especially after the suspension of specie payments in France at the time of the Franco-Prussian War. He says, in "Lombard Street:" —

"Formerly, for many purposes, Paris was a European settling-house; but now it has ceased to be so. The note of the Bank of France has not indeed been depreciated enough to disorder ordinary transactions; but any depreciation, however small, — even the liability to depreciation without its reality, — is enough to disorder exchange transactions; they are calculated to such an extremity of fineness that the change of a decimal may be fatal, and may turn a profit into a loss. Accordingly, London has become the sole great settling-house of exchange transactions in Europe."

A banking system capable of conducting great transactions through branches in all parts of the world is almost as essential to financial supremacy as a definite monetary standard. Great Britain owes a large share of her power to the generosity with which she has chartered the great foreign banks with London branches and the London banks with foreign branches, whose capital, amounting to $345,000,000, has already been mentioned. These banks are distinct from those which carry on the domestic banking of the kingdom. The joint stock banks of England and Wales number only 90; but their nearly six thousand branches throughout the kingdom have secured them deposits of nearly $3,000,000,000. The rapidity with which capitalization proceeds under such conditions is indicated by the fact that these deposits have nearly doubled since 1888. Moreover, they do not include the deposits in the post-office savings banks, which increased from £53,974,065, at the close of 1887, to £115,896,786 ($570,000,000), at the close of 1897. The permission to establish branches, which is accorded to all the great British banks, has done much to accumulate the capital of the community in their hands, and to turn it to the most productive uses at home and abroad. In the United States, branch banking would do much toward producing the same results. It is also desirable that banks should be permitted to issue their credits in the form most convenient to their patrons. The issue of notes is the most acceptable form of issuing credit in many parts of the United States; and a more elastic note system is of the first importance, if American banks are to be enabled to reduce their charges to the lowest limit and to compete successfully with their great European rivals.

Old restrictions upon trade, and useless superstitions, must be abandoned in the contest for commercial supremacy. The policy of protection must be adapted by its friends to the new conditions, or it must be abandoned. Protection may be useful in stimulating infant industries: it becomes a relic of mediævalism when it stimulates production which has already become excessive, and which can find an outlet only in a field which protection cannot enter. The political organization of the country should also be given a degree of harmony and symmetry which will permit the direction of the whole power of the state toward definite and intelligent policies. This is one of the secrets of the success of the Russian government, with its absolute power, and, in a lesser degree, of the success of the British Empire, which has steadily maintained the colonial policy of Great Britain where the British flag has once been raised, with only such changes under successive administrations as modern progress has seemed to require. Party politics have not paralyzed British power, because the executive and legislative branches of the government have been in harmony, and because an imperial policy has seldom been antagonized upon petty partisan grounds.

If the American Constitution, framed for conditions more different, from an economic standpoint, from those of the present than the difference between the times of Augustus and those of Jefferson, requires amendment, in order to consolidate the industrial and financial resources of the Union to meet her rivals as a world power, the Constitution, like other human instruments, should be amended. This has been the secret of the preservation of the British Constitution. It has not been a set of rigid formulas inscribed upon mouldering parchment. The constitution has kept pace with the steady upward march of the British people, from the days when the barons wrung Magna Charta from King John, nearly seven centuries ago, to the modern development of free suffrage at home, of supreme power on the ocean, and of the ability to dictate financial policies to the world; and its expansion to meet new necessities has never failed to respond to the enlightened judgment of the directors of Britain's imperial policy.

IV

CAN NEW OPENINGS BE FOUND FOR CAPITAL?

The question which is forcing itself home upon every civilized people to-day is, where openings are to be found in the future for the productive investment of their saved capital. For a score of years there has been a tendency toward higher prices for first-class securities and a diminishing return upon investments. Only within the past two years have higher discount rates appeared in Germany and other continental countries, raising the hope that new fields for investment were absorbing a part of surplus capital. The vital question was discussed with much learning at the January meeting of the Society of Political Economy at Paris, whether this relief was permanent, or was only an eddy in the downward course of the rate of interest. It was pointed out by Professor Clément Juglar that, while many European securities were selling at prices lower than when they were issued a few years ago, indicating a rise in their interest-paying value, the return upon Australian and American securities had permanently fallen from six to four per cent.

The discussion of the small returns upon saved capital and the absolute necessity for new opportunities for its investment marks an important turning-point in economic history. It is not the first time that the supply of capital has outrun the limits of effective demand in sound investments, and has by its excess forced down the interest rate to a point which has caused heavy losses and alarm among the owners of capital. The economic history of the world has afforded several periods of congestion of this sort, when it seemed that savings must be relaxed or new outlets for them found, unless the point of saturation was to be reached for saved capital, and state socialism was to supersede the system of private saving. The congestion has on previous occasions reduced interest rates as low as those of the last few years, but never before has the accumulation of capital been so enormous, nor have so many millions of individuals — those of modest means as well as the typical "capitalist" of socialistic dreams — been confronted by the condition that their savings must be greatly multiplied in order to afford the old return, and that even such savings as they had could with difficulty find safe lodgment in productive enterprises.

The essential question of the future, regarding the great accumulations of saved capital, is whether they shall continue to depress interest rates to the vanishing-point, and at the same time create such a competition for safe investments that a large proportion of the world's savings will be stolen by company promoters and swallowed up in unproductive enterprises. The mere reduction of the returns upon saved capital offers in itself a serious social problem, independent of the danger of unsound investments and the loss of savings. If the savings of a lifetime have heretofore been just sufficient, with interest at six per cent., to afford a comfortable maintenance for old age, they will prove pitifully insufficient with interest reduced to three per cent., and inadequate to avert destitution if interest should fall to one or one and a half per cent., as has seemed among the possibilities of the future. The necessary saving in capital would be four times greater, in order to obtain a comfortable maintenance, with interest at one and a half per cent. than at six per cent.

While the increased earning power of civilized men by means of machinery would bridge a part of this chasm, it would not solve the problem. If it should become practically impossible for persons of small and moderate earnings to save enough during their years of active life to provide for their years of decline, the civilized world would confront the problem whether saving for investment, among the laboring masses at least, should not be abandoned, and the support of old age derived entirely from current taxation. Such a moderate step as this in state socialism — already well under way in Germany, and seriously discussed in Great Britain — might avert for many generations the congestion and consolidation of capital without shaking the pillars of the existing social system.

It is proper to inquire, whether there is not a prospect that new openings will be found for saved capital in the future without the reconstruction of society. An answer in the affirmative can probably be given as to the immediate future, and perhaps as far into the future as it is necessary for human foresight to penetrate. It is essential that these new openings should be important enough to absorb considerable amounts of saved capital beyond the demands for the mere maintenance of existing means of production, and the incidental improvements in them which are required from time to time. It is not probable that the new openings will be sufficient to raise permanently the rate of interest in the near future; but they may stay its downward course. M. Paul Leroy-Beaulieu, in discussing this subject in "l'Economiste Français" of January 28, 1899, calls attention to the fact that there were interruptions in the downward course of interest when steam came to be generally employed as a motive power between 1850 and 1865, and again after the great destruction of capital in the Franco-Prussian war. But, he declares, "after each of these interruptions, the rate of interest again tended to decline to a level lower than before; so that, in taking as the point of departure the beginning of the last quarter century or that of the last half century, — the year 1874 or the year 1850, — it may be noted that the rate of interest has considerably fallen, not in a straight line, it is true, but in a broken line, and that never in our history was it as low as in 1897."

A reason for believing that openings for saved capital may be found in the immediate future without the reconstruction of society is the fact that such periods of congestion have occurred before, but have been terminated by new demands for capital, caused by discoveries in the field of invention or by territorial acquisition. The world may continue for many centuries to go through the process of capitalization, consolidation, and the shifting to new peoples of commercial supremacy without the abandonment of the institution of private property, which seems so essential to individual ambition and national achievement. The fall in the earning power of capital permits the substitution of mechanical devices for human labor whenever the interest upon the capital required for a new improvement falls below the cost of the labor which it replaces. Thus fields are opened for capital which remained closed while labor was the cheaper instrument, and the labor released is free to seek higher employments. Machinery, which is the fruit of saved capital, thus invades new fields not only with the reduction in the price of its manufacture, but with the fall in the rental cost of the capital invested in it.

The accumulation of saved capital is now so much more rapid than it was even a quarter of a century ago, and the world is so much more completely equipped with the mechanism of production, that something more than a new invention or an important war will be required permanently to raise the rate of interest. There are indications, however, of several possible openings which may absorb surplus savings and afford a moderate return upon capital for several decades to come. One of these is the general application of electricity as a motive power; a second is the extension of railways over the undeveloped countries of Africa and Asia; and a third is the equipment of these countries with the machinery of production. These openings for capital promise to absorb many millions within the next ten or twenty years. Prior to the extension of European influence in Africa and recent development in China, society was reaching the state of economic congestion portrayed by Mr. Brooks Adams in his interesting work, "The Law of Civilization and Decay," and his more recent article in the "Fortnightly Review" for February, 1899, on "The New Struggle for Life among the Nations." The congestion has not, as he seems to believe, very much to do with the supply of gold and silver, the mere tools of exchange; it has to do with the subject of exchange, — the great mass of capital seeking employment, and unable to find it at home.

A congestion of capital of serious proportions was threatened during the third and fourth decades of the century, as the result of the favorable conditions of civil order and the growing use of labor-saving machinery in the textile industries which followed the Napoleonic wars. There appeared suddenly, however, several great outlets for saved capital. The most conspicuous was the building of railways, which demanded hundreds of millions, first in England and France, then in America, and finally in the countries of Eastern Europe, South America, Australia, and India. Interest rates rose under the pressure of active demand for capital, and the outlook was again rosy for the profitable use of savings, whether of the laborer or the merchant prince.

Two powerful influences in accelerating the growth of available capital came into operation by the middle of the century,—the full organization of credit and the development of machine production. The extension of machine production so increased the power of the individual arm that if savings were possible under the old conditions of hand labor, the capacity for them became many times as great under the new conditions of machine production. These savings in the early years had lain idle in old stockings and bureau drawers. They were largely made in gold or silver, withdrawing from active use without interest a part of the capital produced by arduous labor in the mines. But the banks of England and France, which had stood almost alone down to 1850, were about that time imitated all over Europe. Belgium was dowered with a national bank; banks sprung up in Spain, in Italy, in the little states of Switzerland, and all over Germany; while in England and France the great monopoly banks of issue witnessed the growth of potent rivals in the joint stock banks and the credit societies.

Savings which, under earlier conditions, had lain idle, until perhaps an amount equal to their entire value was consumed in the interest lost, became, under the new system, immediately available for increasing the machinery of production and exchange at home, and swelling the fund to be loaned to new countries for the creation of railways, steamships, cotton mills, and public works. To put into mathematics the greater potency of a given unit of saved capital under the new system, and then to multiply this by the constantly accelerating savings, is hardly within the limits of human capacity; but it is obvious that the slow accumulations which had gone on in early centuries were now multiplied almost in a geometrical ratio as the increased savings of one year went to develop the capacity for saving by the growth of machine plants and means of communication in the years which followed.

It is not surprising that economic crises of the gravest character have grown out of forced adjustments to the new conditions. Consumption has far from kept pace with increased production. The average man of small means, content to live from hand to mouth a century ago, has become a capitalist, a contributor toward the construction of railways in South America, Asia, and Africa, and a bidder on the world's exchanges for national and industrial securities against the sons of the great Jewish bankers of the last century.

Capital can be saved only in gold, in consumable goods, or in those permanent contributions to the machinery of production,—buildings, tools, and improvements — which are happily described by French economists as *installations*. The saving of capital in gold has practically ceased. The saving of consumable goods is practiced only to the extent that they are needed for immediate wants and in current processes of production. The saving of capital in permanent works has found an expanding outlet as new methods of machine production have been devised, as increasing wealth has developed new wants, and as the State has availed herself of the growing wealth of the community to create highways, bridges, railways, harbors, and public buildings for the benefit of all. But these outlets have threatened for a moment to be choked. The rate of interest, in orderly societies, is the measure of the relation of supply of capital to the demand for it, and this rate has indicated in recent years a constantly increasing supply in proportion to the legitimate demand for productive purposes.

The saving of capital in permanent form has been greatly promoted by the issue of negotiable securities. These instruments have given a transferable character, approximating that of money, to property in almost all productive enterprises, because they have, like money, established a common denominator in which such values might be expressed and transferred. So long as new productive enterprises can be created by means of stock companies, the capital of the individual flows readily from the reservoirs of his own saving into the great channels of loanable capital. The difficulty which is disclosed at a certain stage of social development is an excess of saved capital over the opportunities for safe investment.

There is little doubt that the owners of capital are intelligent enough, upon the average, to invest their savings chiefly in productive enterprises rather than unproductive ones, while the productive enterprises constitute the chief means of investment. The prevalence of abuses in company promotion, great losses in unproductive enterprises, and the persistent flotation of the stocks and bonds of projects which afford no real promise of adequate returns, are not the results of a sudden accession of rascality in human nature, but merely of the great excess of saved capital seeking investment over safe and profitable outlets.

An interesting proof that the supply of capital has become so excessive that it is simply doubling upon itself without profit to its owners is afforded by the conversions of government, railway, and industrial securities in Europe during the last few years. M. Georges de Laveleye, who presents annually in the "Moniteur des Intérêts Matériels" of Brussels a statement of all the issues of negotiable securities for the year, expressed the opinion in 1892 that Europe was capable of absorbing from four to five thousand millions of francs in new securities upon the average each year. The average issues from 1886 to 1890 were 8,070,000,000 francs, and M. de Laveleye came to the conclusion that this was an excessive movement, and would involve losses and liquidations. The issues from 1891 to 1895, inclusive, fell within his limit of the digestive capacity of European capital, but 1896 showed net issues, exclusive of conversions, amounting to 9,129,054,150 francs; 1897 showed issues of 8,911,870,530 francs, and 1898 issues of 8,902,776,660. It is the conversions which throw the most searching light upon the problem of excessive savings. These conversions amounted in 1894 to 12,641,200,000 francs ($2,450,000,000), or more than double the issues for new enterprises, and they amounted in 1896 to 7,593,013,475 francs ($1,465,000,000).

The remarkable fact connected with the conversions of 1894 was that the saving in interest to the issuers of the securities was 119,433,000 francs ($23,000,000) a year, and this saving was sufficient to pay the interest on all the new issues upon a two and a half per cent. basis. In other words, the savings of capital in Europe and other civilized countries in 1894, applied to the purchase of new securities to the amount of $1,000,000,000 (5,173,448,035 francs), were absorbed without increasing the earning power of the capital invested. The situation in 1896 was not quite so barren for investors, but the conversions effected afforded a saving to the issuers of securities to the amount of 40,000,000 francs ($7,740,000) a year. The conversions of five per cent. obligations to four per cent. in 1894 were 3,145,000,000 francs ($600,000,000), and the conversions of four and a half per cent. obligations upon a three per cent. basis were 7,000,000,000 francs ($1,350,000,000). Most of the obligations of solvent states and corporations have been reduced to four per cent. or less, and their actual return to the investor at market prices, in spite of some recent fluctuations, has tended toward two and a half per cent.

Strong proof that the United States have reached the state of excessive capitalization, unable to find productive investment at home in new enterprises, is afforded by the recent activity in floating the securities of industrial trusts, and by the piling up of unused funds in the banks. The common and preferred stock of trust combinations, organized and proposed during 1898, was given by the "United States Investor" of February 11, 1899, as $1,725,099,200, while additions to the list in the first two months of 1899, of $844,800,000, carried the total for fourteen months to $2,569,899,200. These great combinations and issues of securities are symptomatic of two things, — the tendency to arrest overproduction and ruinous competition by limiting production, and the eagerness of promoters to take advantage of the masses of idle capital seeking investment to transfer a part of it to their own pockets.

Let us turn to the three suggested openings for the great mass of saved capital seeking investment, and consider how great an outlet they afford, and how important it is that they should not be closed to the capital and enterprise of the great producing countries. The three outlets named were the application of electricity to motive power, the building of railways in undeveloped countries, and the further equipment of such countries with the machinery of production and intercommunication.

It is obvious that capital should be given free entrance into all these fields, in order that it may not be shut up to feeding upon itself, without increased earning power, as is coming to be the case in the great capitalistic countries. Protective tariffs have not heretofore been raised against capital, and the countries most in need of development are not likely to bar foreign capital of their own motion from their limits. But capital as well as trade "follows the flag" to a large extent, because under the flag of its own government, or that of some civilized and responsible state, it finds the guarantee of security and respect for contracts which make possible safe investments and uninterrupted industrial and commercial growth.

The application of electricity to motive power is likely to absorb a large amount of capital within the next one or two decades, without involving considerations of national policy. The railways of the world, with a capital estimated by Mr. Mullhall in 1894 at £6,745,000,000, may be called upon to replace that portion of their capital invested in locomotives by new machinery at a cost of several thousand millions of dollars. The creation of electric street-car lines is already extending over Europe, and M. Fournier de Flaix declared, in the "Revue des Banques" for November, 1898, that the Paris Exposition of 1900 would draw its chief attraction from the various modes of applying electricity to locomotion and production.

Statistics at the beginning of 1898 showed 2289 kilometres (1420 miles) of electric roads in Europe, with 4514 motors. The General Electric Company of Germany now employs 12,000 persons, and during 1898 increased its trackage 329 kilometres, and the number of its cars from 1343 to 1861. The capital for these enterprises has already been obtained without any marked effect upon the existing supply seeking investment; but this is only the beginning, and while the change from steam to electric power will come gradually, and will be met to some extent out of railway and factory earnings, the demand for capital for this purpose may be more potent than any single mechanical change within the present generation.

The building of railways in undeveloped countries seems likely to attain within a short time an extension and importance almost equal to the great outbreak of railway building activity between 1850 and 1870. That phenomenon promoted the creation of banks and finance companies, and absorbed capital so rapidly as to raise the rate of interest materially above that which prevailed when Great Britain was loaning her surplus capital, early in the century, to the new countries of South America.

The trans-Siberian railway, already well advanced toward completion by the Russian government, and projected to stretch over 4200 miles from the Ural Mountains to the Pacific Ocean, is the pioneer among the intercontinental lines. The government had already expended upon it, up to the close of 1897, $188,000,000. The construction of the trans-Saharian across "the Great Desert," binding the French province of Algiers to the French colonies in Central Africa, is one of the dreams of French economists and statesmen which seems upon the point of being put into practical form. Englishmen in Egypt and South Africa are urging the creation of a line "from Cairo to the Cape," which will almost equal the trans-Siberian in its length, and will surpass it in the savage character of the country through which it will pass. Concessions have been granted by the Turkish government for a line from Tripoli on the Mediterranean to the Persian Gulf, with branches extending into Persia, which will reduce by five days the time between Brindisi in southern Italy and Bombay in the heart of India. Extensions of this line might afford a powerful counterpoise to the trans-Siberian, and increase the facilities of England for protecting her Indian empire against Russian aggression on the north.

China is on the point of being gridironed with the means of railway transportation. It is the result of inevitable economic tendencies that Great Britain, France, Germany, and Russia have been contending for the privilege of advancing the capital for these great works, and have almost gone to war for the political preponderance and commercial influence which this privilege involves. A recent publication of the Prussian government sets forth that Asia, the greatest of the continents and the most largely peopled, has but 26,890 miles of railway, — about one sixteenth of the mileage of the world. This condition is rapidly changing. A list of operating and projected lines in China, in the "Revue des Banques" for November, 1898, names six lines under English control, one Anglo-German, one Anglo-Italian, two German, four French, one Franco-Belgian, and four Russian lines, including the sections of the trans-Siberian. The construction of these lines will call for many millions of British, French, German, and American savings, and will help to postpone the further fall in the rate of interest. It is doubtful, however, whether all these lines will at once prove remunerative, and whether investors will not suffer again some of the losses which resulted from British investments in South America in the twenties, and from later ventures in American railways, Australian banks and land, and Western farm mortgages.

Those investors are likely to be safest who have a government guarantee, by means of a public loan, for the interest on the investment, whether the particular enterprise for which the loan is placed proves successful or not. An important feature of the present policy for finding safe investments for national capital is the control of the field of investment by responsible governments.

Many of the great loans in new countries, early in the century, and even down to recent times, like those in the Argentine Republic and Hayti, have been made chiefly to revolutionary governments, where unwise financiering, official corruption, and the adoption of an irredeemable paper currency have wrecked business and frightened away foreign capital. A new era is opening for such investments, under the protection of responsible powers, whether a direct guarantee of the interest is given by the powers themselves, or reliance is placed upon the governing capacity of the men of the Anglo-Saxon or other European races, who exercise indirectly the control over the finances of the protected country. Already the powers have intervened in Egypt and Greece for the creation of boards of control, which see to it that the taxes are honestly collected, that the interest on the public debt is paid, and that the funds obtained are not diverted from their proper uses to the pockets of corrupt officials.

Egypt was found by the powers a financial wreck in 1881, but under the efficient direction of Lord Cromer, British adviser of the Khedive, Egyptian securities have become among the safest which are quoted on European bourses. At the close of the war with Turkey Greece found herself practically bankrupt, with her securities depreciated, and her forced paper currency at a heavier discount than before the war. The intervention of Great Britain, France, and Russia, with the appointment of a board of control to supervise the proper collection of the taxes and the payment of interest on the debt, promptly put her upon a solvent basis. A loan of 155,000,000 francs ($30,000,000) was issued under the guarantee of the three powers, at the rate of two and a half per cent., upon which a slight premium was charged. Notwithstanding this low return upon the capital invested, the amount offered at Paris — 41,500,000 francs ($8,000,000) — was subscribed twenty-three times over by 1387 subscribers. The deposits made on behalf of subscribers at the Bank of France were 196,579,000 francs, and the amounts subscribed for were 987,809,475 francs ($190,000,000). The British government has taken a somewhat different course in regard to its own dependencies by a bill, now pending, to give the guarantee of the home government to the colonial loans of the crown colonies.

All these plans have this feature in common, — that they have behind them the moral support of a great civilized state, capable of protecting the interests of its citizens by force of arms, and ready to do so if occasion requires. The government of adventurers and financial freebooters is coming to an end in Europe, Africa, and Asia, and it may yet be the mission of the United States to bring it to an end in portions of Latin America.

Only by the firm hand of the responsible governing races, as Mr. Benjamin Kidd has so forcibly pointed out in his thoughtful works on social development, can the assurance of uninterrupted progress be conveyed to the tropical and undeveloped countries. This duty, imposed upon the superior races by the evolution of events, if not by the moral order, affords the opportunity for the absorption of the surplus of savings not applied to current consumption which is going on under the existing social system. Those who do not welcome the responsibilities and the opportunity which this situation creates are fostering the discontent within the old civilized countries which breeds social and political revolution. The excess of production of finished goods over effective demand, the creation of trust combinations to check production, the resulting reductions of wages and of opportunity for the employment of labor, — all these are the consequences of shutting up capital to feed upon itself by closing the fields for new investments.

The present production of finished goods far outruns the effective demand, and the investment of saved capital in new manufacturing plants in the producing countries simply divides or destroys the small profits heretofore earned by the existing establishments. The owners of these plants are in many cases widows, orphans, and those of small means who are trying to save for a rainy day. They suffer more by the failure of manufacturing and railway dividends than the princes of industry and finance. The latter are usually able to take care of themselves, by such projects as the present multiplication of trust syndicates, whose securities can be unloaded upon the small investor before their overcapitalization and barrenness of productive power are ascertained.

Trust combinations for limiting production and reducing the number and wages of the employed are the only safeguard against destructive competition and the ruin of the less perfected manufacturing plants, so long as outlets cannot be found for saved capital in countries whose producing plant and means of communication are not yet substantially complete. It is useless to say that the capital might be employed productively at home under existing conditions. It could be thus employed if saving were checked, and the money now directed toward investments were applied to the purchase of consumable goods. But such a change in the conduct of the governing races means a reversal of the lessons taught by five centuries of civilization; it means the serious modification of the present social order, and the adoption of old-age pensions and other devices for applying the results of current production to consumption instead of saving for the future.

The opponents of the intervention of the civilized countries in the undeveloped countries perpetually discuss the position of the supporters of intervention, as if the entire demand on their part were for new markets for finished goods, and point out with truth that the equipment of the new countries with the machinery of production tends to narrow the market for the finished products of the old countries. But this is setting up and knocking down a man of straw. The benefits to the old countries in the control of the undeveloped countries do not lie chiefly in the outlet for consumable goods. It is precisely to escape the necessity for the reduplication of the plants which produce the goods, by finding a field elsewhere for the creation of new plants, including not only competing machinery, but the highways of commerce, — railways, roads, canals, and improved harbors, — that the savings of the capitalistic countries are seeking an outlet beyond their own limits. It is not the assurance that more goods can be sold which is needed by the manufacturer so much as the assurance that perpetually increasing savings shall not bid against his present production in his own market, by the creation of rival plants, equipped with every improvement of modern machinery. Incidentally and for a time, political dependencies and "spheres of influence" afford an enlarged market for finished goods; but the essential benefit of such openings is the opportunity which they present, under the guarantee of order and the sanctity of contracts, for the productive use of the surplus savings of the masses of the people — laboring men, small merchants, and professional men, as well as great capitalists.

The question may naturally be asked — and has been asked by those who can make no other answer to this argument — whether this requirement of new countries for the employment of saved capital does not bring the human race to a jumping-off place as soon as Africa and Asia are capitalized by the extraordinarily rapid processes which have marked the capitalization of the western part of the United States, Germany, and Russia. This question looks too far into the future to be capable of a precise answer. It does not necessarily follow, however, from the congestion of capital which appears to exist to-day, that conditions may not arise within another generation which will work a revolution in the conditions of production. It may be suggested, at the risk of penetrating into the domain of the fanciful, that when the food-supplying area of the world becomes circumscribed in proportion to population, — as Mr. John Hyde pointed out, in the "North American Review" for February, 1899, might be the case in the United States in less than half a century, — great demands for capital may arise for the production of food by chemical processes. Already distinguished chemists are dreaming of an era when chemistry shall banish agriculture from the field and farm, and when the interior heat of the earth and the warmth of the sun shall be utilized to obtain the power now derived from the rapidly shrinking coal supply.

The present generation cannot grapple with these problems, and is not required to. Thus far in the history of the world, mechanical inventions, chemical discoveries, and the development of the mechanism of money and credit have barely kept pace with the imperative needs of human society. Inventions and discoveries which are not yet needed fall upon an unheeding world. The inventors and discoverers go to neglected graves, and wait for later generations to do them justice.

The present generation can face only the problems at hand, and the opportunities at hand for the maintenance of its own social system. These opportunities embrace the equipment of the whole world with a producing plant, and with means of communication and exchange, which will raise the undeveloped portions, as far as may be, to the level of comfort, producing power, and civilization of the more advanced portions. This is the mission of the great civilized states to-day; and those states which timidly withdraw from competition with powerful rivals, either from defects in their political system or lack of commercial energy, will sentence themselves to the fate of the decadent countries, like Persia, Turkey, and Spain, — once masters of the world, but now the victims of the greater energy and foresight of the northern races.

V

THE NEW ECONOMIC PROBLEMS

THE events of the last decade, and particularly of the last few years, have required a readjustment by economic thinkers of many preconceived points of view upon important subjects relating to industry and capital. It is not so much that the maxims of classical political economy have been proven false, as that those upon which stress has been laid during the effort to emancipate industry from mediæval fetters have become of subordinate importance because their operation has come to be modified by new conditions.

The last few years have witnessed a remarkable expansion in trade and industry in nearly every civilized country, which is causing a larger volume of production in proportion to population, and employing a larger capital than any previous development of the kind. The rate for the rental of capital has risen upon every European money market higher than for many years. The great increase in the gold supply, which has added $700,000,000, or nearly twenty-five per cent., to the gold currency of the world since 1892, seems to have been ineffective in arresting the scarcity of money. Prices of commodities have risen in a surprising degree, and mills and factories have orders which cannot be filled for many months.

While this revival of industry, following upon the panic of 1893, bears much resemblance to the revivals that have followed earlier periods of depression, an important new element has gradually become a controlling factor in the situation. This is the widening of the field of competition. This widening of the field has proceeded with accelerating pace during the last two centuries as the result of labor-saving machinery, swift and cheap methods of communication, and the great accumulations of saved capital resulting from the use of these improved instruments of production and exchange. The widening of the field of effective competitors first brought the producer into competition with his near neighbors, then with the producers of the whole nation, and finally with foreign competitors on a limited scale on his own soil. The condition which now confronts him is the necessity of seeking new outlets, whether for finished goods or saved capital, in foreign markets, where he must compete with other producers from without who have entered the field under the same stimulus as himself. This stimulus is the persistent human motive of the struggle for existence, and in this struggle no practical formula has yet been found to supersede that of "the survival of the fittest."

These new conditions of world competition do not permit effective aid to the producer by favoring legislation at home, except such as carefully removes restrictions upon the economy and efficiency of production. The home market is more than supplied by the existing equipment of machinery and capital. The new market opening in the undeveloped countries will be won by the people showing the greatest efficiency in every department of production, — not merely in machinery and labor, but in the organization of their banking and carrying systems and their distribution of the burdens of taxation. Local markets have been merged into a world market, where the operator in goods, money, or securities can place orders or make sales at his will, in London, Paris, Vienna, or New York, according as the news brought by telegraph, telephone, or cable indicates that he can buy cheaper or sell dearer at any given moment.

It is in this world market that the manufacturers and capitalists of the United States, as well as those of England and continental Europe, must hereafter compete with one another. Powerful influences have swept away the natural barriers to competition by making it possible to transfer goods at small cost from the place of production to the remote corners of the world. The reduction of railway charges and ocean freights has followed the multiplication of lines of transportation and economies in railway management and steamship construction. One of the most serious problems of railway competition at the present day is the adjustment of rates that shall be fair between communities which at widely varying distances claim the right to lay down their products upon equal terms in the same market. The difference of a few cents per box may determine whether California, or Florida, or Jamaica, shall control the market for oranges in New York. A similar difference in freight from the West, as between New York or Newport News, may determine which city shall be the commercial emporium of the Western world. The breadth of the Atlantic is made "a negligible quality" by "export rates" which impose the same charges upon freight from the Mississippi to Europe that are made from the Mississippi to New York.

The railway may thus, in a more emphatic sense than ever before, annihilate distances which exist; it also has the power to lengthen distances for all competitive purposes by hostile rates. These mighty engines of competition, hitherto restricted in the main to Europe and America, are putting "a girdle round about the earth." They are traversing the steppes whose sombre silence has been broken for centuries only by the horses' hoofs of Tartar robbers, or by the march of the armed servants of Russian despotism; they are marking China into a checkerboard by bands of steel; they are preparing to link northern and southern Africa together "from Cairo to the Cape," and across the Desert of Sahara; and their victorious march from

Asia Minor across the valleys of the Tigris and Euphrates to the confines of India promises a more enduring conquest for civilization than that of Alexander's armies. Under their competition the possibility of finding an exclusive market and retaining it against rivals by the barriers of distance and difficulty of approach is becoming as vain as the search of the alchemist for the source of gold, or the quest of Ponce de Leon for the fountain of perpetual youth.

One of the facts that has contributed to the merging of local markets into a world market, and has changed the bearings of some of the propositions of classical political economy toward the modern world, is the great accumulation of saved capital. This fact has resulted in a permanent decline of the rate of interest on capital, in spite of the fluctuations of the discount rate which have for the moment carried the rental price of currency to a high figure. Saving now finds little outlet, except in duplicating needlessly the existing machinery of production and transportation, or extending it in directions where an immediate return in the form of dividends is not assured.

The reduction in the rate of profit from savings should have the effect, according to the play of classical economic laws, to diminish saving on the one hand, and by the lower rental value of capital make many enterprises practicable which were not so when the rental of capital was high. It is doubtful if the first of these supposed effects of low interest — the diminution of saving — will be felt to any serious extent in modern society. The instinct of saving is to a considerable degree independent of the earning of dividends. Hoards of gold and silver are common among the people of India and other half-civilized countries, where the capital lies buried in some hiding-place without yielding a penny of return. The expectation of dividends from investment is a modern phenomenon, which is only one phase of the passion for saving instilled by the evolution of civilized society. Even if the tendency to saving might be somewhat impaired by diminished returns, there is a counter influence in the necessity for larger savings than before to obtain a given return, and there is a constant addition to the number of those making savings under the tendency of growing social wealth to swell the numbers of the well-to-do classes, and diminish the proportion of those in the lower economic strata.

The diversion of capital to enterprises which would never have been executed under high rates for money is undoubtedly an important factor in absorbing the surplus of savings in modern society. Enterprises which would not have been thought possible a generation or two ago are now boldly taken up and carried through by private individuals and the state. Where such enterprises, however, supplant hand labor by the economy of machine production, the saving power of society is again increased, and the absorption of capital in these new directions is offset by the new capital created and the labor released for other productive employments. Upon the whole, therefore, the opportunity for the absorption of the savings now going on in civilized society, in such a manner as to yield dividends upon investments, must evidently be found in countries that lack the equipment of Western civilization.

There are great risks involved in such investments, because of the necessarily speculative character of enterprises which strike out in new paths. Mistakes must almost inevitably be made in regard to supply and demand in adapting to new peoples the mechanism which has met the needs of older civilizations. Great Britain, the first of the modern capitalistic states to make loans abroad, discovered these dangers when millions were swallowed up in the panic of 1825 by bad investments in Latin America, and again in 1857 by the overcapitalization of American railways; but neither these experiences, nor the reckless advances of the Barings in Argentina, which culminated in the crisis of 1890, nor the locking up of Scottish funds in Australia in 1893, have diverted English capital permanently from the hopeful channels opened for its investment in undeveloped countries.

The surplus of saved capital in modern society threatens to impair the force of the classical theories regarding expenditure by the state. Economists have for many years protested against the astonishing growth in public expenditure and the negotiation of loans to meet it. They have denounced in the strongest terms the doctrines that a public loan was only the transfer of the people's money from one pocket to the other, and left the state no poorer than before. The classical theories are indisputably correct when applied to the relative poverty of society two or three generations ago, or when directed against a policy which handicaps competing power by taxing industry unduly to maintain an overgrown military establishment. From a philosophical point of view, however, the increase in state expenditure appears to be a normal development resulting from the evolution of modern society. The primary cause is the great increase in wealth, which permits the citizen to give up to the state, without feeling the burden, many times the amount that drove the subjects of Charles I. to rebellion, or impoverished France before the Revolution. Growing out of this increase of wealth are the double influences of a greater subdivision of labor, which throws upon the state many new functions, without at all implying a direct progress toward socialism, and the birth of enterprises looking too far into the future to attract individual capital by the promise of an early return.

The growth of social wealth permits additions to the professional and office-holding classes of the community in a constantly accelerating ratio. If the producing power of the community is barely sufficient to supply food, clothing, and shelter, the amount of the annual earnings that can be set aside for the employment of physicians, lawyers, theatrical performers, singers, and authors is extremely small. If these classes exist, they will live the precarious livelihood of the hack writers and strolling performers of a century or two ago. When, however, the rate of production in a community is such as to afford a surplus of capital above the amount required for the necessaries of life, the professional and office-holding classes will receive a large proportion of this surplus. The better care of health will afford employment for physicians, the management of property will give rise to litigation and afford incomes to lawyers and bankers, amusements will be more largely patronized to the benefit of actors and singers, more books will be bought to the profit of publishers and authors, and the payment of generous prices for works of art will make possible a prosperous class of sculptors and painters. Under such conditions the people will look without impatience upon expenditures by the state for libraries, works of art, and the many branches of scientific investigation which are now pursued by civilized governments. The rise of the standard of living, moreover, will be accompanied by higher salaries in official places, and will swell the budget of the state far beyond its amount in earlier and poorer times.

The subdivision of labor imposes new functions upon a state, largely because the individual citizen, absorbed in his own special work by the exacting conditions of the new competition, is debarred from that general knowledge of markets, qualities of goods, and prices which was possible for his ancestors. Whatever may be the ultimate tendency of such legislation in paving the way toward socialism, it cannot be treated in its essence as socialistic nor as abridging the freedom of the citizen. The citizen simply delegates to his servants, intelligent specialists in official employ, the functions which in a more primitive state he exercised for himself, but with much less expert knowledge and efficiency.

It is not necessary to carry the illustration of these functions into great detail, in order to indicate how largely responsible they are for the increase of official budgets so much bewailed by some of the classical economists. Many of these expenditures by the state, such as those for food inspection, street cleaning, and garbage collecting, are nothing more than the delegation of small items of individual expenditure to public officials, who, by means of the concentration of the work, and in spite of the admitted inefficiency of officialdom, render services at small cost which would otherwise wastefully absorb the time, thought, and money of individuals.

Coming to the broader problem of state expenditures for important public works, it is obvious that there are many such works which are not attractive to private capital, because of the delay in reaping the profits from them, but which will afford a substantial net gain to the community within a reasonable period. The works of this class are those requiring a good many years of preparation before the results are realized, — what the French call works *de longue haleine*. For such works the state is undoubtedly justified in negotiating loans, if the benefits of the undertaking are plainly shown. There are also classes of works whose benefits to the community as a whole are plain, and may even involve the question of its supremacy in commercial competition with other communities, but whose benefits are so minutely subdivided that they cannot well be made the subject of definite charges.

Among the first of these classes of works are canals and railways in countries capable of development, but not promising immediate returns to private investors at the rates which a railway would be permitted to charge. Such enterprises are not economically justifiable if they do not afford an economy over preëxisting methods; but railways are compelled to make their charges upon a basis fixed by custom rather than just within the limits of the old charges for wagon or water service. In the second class may be found river and harbor improvements, which may be of great value to the community, but whose benefits might be neutralized if heavy tolls were levied either by a private corporation or by the state.

The ultimate test of the wisdom of any work intended purely for utility should be its dividend-paying capacity, if the dividend can be collected from all who benefit by it; but where a community possesses sufficient surplus wealth to accomplish important improvements, it may be simpler and more economical to distribute the benefits by taxation over the whole community than to attempt to divide them into specific tolls of infinitesimal amount and inquisitorial character.

While these considerations appear to justify some relaxation of the rigid enforcement of the doctrines of *laissez faire*, there is no doubt that state expenditures and state intervention in private affairs are liable to grave abuses. The most severe scrutiny both as to objects and as to methods of state expenditure should not be relaxed, because the principle is admitted that state action may be justified. In other words, the burden of proof should continue to rest upon those who ask for state interference or state expenditure in any given case, but the case should not be closed to argument upon the theory that the action of the state could not under any conditions be defended, even if substantial benefits to the community by its action should be clearly shown.

The reduction of the return upon investments raises a serious question, as has already been suggested, whether a system of old-age insurance will not soon supersede direct savings for old age by the working classes. There is some danger in applying to the earnings of the people a system of taxation which may make production more costly than that of competing nations, but Germany has already taken some long steps toward old-age insurance, and Great Britain is seriously considering the subject. There is an economic advantage in this measure, in relieving the congestion of capital, because the amount required to support a laborer in old age is taken from current production rather than from the dividends on saved capital. The substitution of the direct method of taxation for the indirect method of saving can hardly diminish in any case the net funds left to the laborer for the purchase of goods for consumption, and is likely materially to increase his capacity for such purchases. The system of saving for investment, with the purpose of applying only the income to maintenance during old age, locks up a much greater amount of capital than would be the case if the active laborers of to-day contributed their share from their current earnings to sustain the retired laborers, and relied upon similar assessments upon the active laborers of the future to sustain them in their old age.

It is probable that the removal of the mass of laborers from the field of those saving for investment would diminish considerably the amount of capital seeking investment on the money market. It would, on the other hand, materially increase the demand for consumption goods. Two or three generations ago such an adjustment of the relations between saving and expenditure would have been a calamity to Western civilization. The character of the problem has been changed by the increase in the amount of saved capital offered annually for investment. These offerings have swelled the supply of such capital beyond the amount that can be profitably invested, and have caused a permanent decline in the rate of interest. The withdrawal of the purchasing power of this savings fund, moreover, from the field of demand for consumption goods has added to the difficulty by diminishing the demand for such goods, while the facilities for producing them were being increased from the savings fund by the duplication of manufacturing plants and lines of transportation.

The natural equilibrium between production and consumption, which is one of the theories of political economy, is based substantially upon the proposition that all that one man produces shall constitute a demand for what others produce. If a portion of one man's purchasing power is withdrawn from the market by being put in the form of a banking credit which is not immediately employed as a demand for other goods, the supply of goods exceeds the effective demand, and this condition is carried in successive waves through every industry, causing overproduction, stagnation, and commercial convulsions. The essential difficulty is that production is diverted by unremunerative investments into wrong channels, and those who have thus employed their savings are deprived at once of the dividends which they expected, and of the comforts they might have enjoyed if they had eschewed saving for the increase of the comforts of life.

The dividing line which shall maintain a really healthy equilibrium between supply and demand is found in an amount of saving sufficient to restore the wear and tear of the existing equipment of production and exchange, provide new equipment for the increase of population and business, and afford a fund of free capital for investment in really profitable new devices for saving labor and increasing production. When the amount of saved capital passes this point, the result is disastrous to individuals, if not to the whole community.

The theory of the classical economy is well founded, that sooner or later society will profit by the reduction of the interest rate, because this reduction will permit the employment of capital in directions where it could not be employed when the rental of capital was high, and will thus increase the sum of comforts placed at the command of the community. Experience has shown, however, that when saved capital accumulates rapidly, the groping after new uses for it, especially within the limits of a well-developed industrial community, causes waste and disaster. The process works with so much friction, and inflicts such severe injury by destroying commercial confidence, arresting production, and thereby throwing laborers out of employment, that checks to the process of capitalization or new outlets for capital must be found to maintain healthy conditions. The establishment of old-age insurance, upon a scale broad enough to divest the system of any aspect of almsgiving and make it a part of the established economic order, would tend to restore the equilibrium between production and consumption by diminishing the amount of new savings seeking investment in fields already occupied.

The appearance of all the great industrial nations in the field of competition for foreign markets imposes upon each the duty of organizing its machinery of competition upon the most economical basis. This requires not merely the adoption of every labor-saving and money-saving device in mechanics and transportation, but the adjustment of the financial and fiscal systems so as to impose the lightest fetters upon industry. Consolidation of small plants is one of the natural results of this new order. This form of organization cannot be carried beyond certain limits without neutralizing its benefits, but within those limits, where combination permits production at diminished cost and economy in distribution, the industrial combination can be stamped out only at the cost of crippling national competing power. It is the widening of markets which is responsible in a large measure for combinations among producers. The trust — where it is a natural economic growth, and not merely a gambling venture by speculators who live by their wits — is simply the combination of several small establishments, in order to secure greater economy and efficiency in the machinery of production. Such economy and efficiency become of the highest importance where more goods are produced at home than can be sold for a profit, and the surplus has to be sold in foreign markets.

The necessity of seeking foreign markets for surplus products operates to some extent to check the power to fix prices far above the point determined by cost of production and legitimate profit. The immunity from competition at home which is secured by the trust, whether under the shelter of special favors by law or not, is lost when its products meet the similar products of other nations in the foreign field. While an international combination in restraint of trade is conceivable, it is not easy to perfect in the case of manufactured goods, in view of differences in language, raw materials, styles, cost of transportation, methods of banking and credit, and the other conditions of production. The price then has to be brought down to the actual competitive price. A surplus may sometimes be unloaded at a lower price abroad than that for which the product is sold at home, but domestic prices must in the long run bear some reasonable relation to foreign prices charged by the same producer for the same goods. In the foreign market, therefore, under modern conditions, the trust combination must prove its right to live by its ability to undersell its rivals. Whatever modification may be required by circumstances in the application of the old doctrines of political economy, there is nothing more true in the long run than the maxim that "speculation succeeds only if it renders a service, — when it has foreseen a future need and satisfied it."

The power of industrial combinations may require regulation by the state for political reasons, but all such regulations should be kept within the narrowest limits which public policy will permit. Taxation should be so adjusted that its burden should not be felt upon the free movement of capital from one industry to another. From this point of view, taxes should be laid upon wealth after it is earned rather than in process of employment as a part of the machinery of production. An income tax, however oppressive its rate, could not essentially change the direction of industry in a given community, because it would fall only upon net profits. If it had any influence in diverting capital from one industry to another, it would have only the legitimate economic influence of reducing the net income of those engaged in the less profitable industries to the point which drove them into the more profitable, and therefore into those to which the natural producing capacity of the country was best adapted. Any tax falling directly upon industry, or upon capital in active use in manufacturing or transportation, even though the net amount exacted from a given individual or corporation were not greater than under the income tax, might give a harmful tendency to the natural direction of capital and industry by falling too lightly on some and too heavily on others.

In the field of finance, the necessity of unfettered movement for the money market and the people who expect to compete successfully with powerful rivals suggests that the fewest possible restrictions should be imposed upon the movement of capital. Taxes upon corporations should be levied upon their net profits rather than upon the transfer of their securities, and the laws regulating the money market should impose no more than a nominal tax upon its transactions.

The wisdom of this rule has been demonstrated within three or four years by the experience of several European money markets. Germany, under the influence of agrarian prejudice against the kings of finance, attempted to crush dealings in futures on the stock exchange and the transfer of securities upon margins. France, under the influence of the official agents of exchange who have for a century had the nominal monopoly of stock exchange operations, imposed restrictions upon the traffic of the unofficial brokers. The result in both cases has been to send a great volume of business to Brussels, where freedom of economic movement is unhampered by restrictive laws. The great Parisian banks have enlarged their branches in Belgium or established new ones, the National Bank of Belgium has become one of the greatest custodians in Europe of private holdings of securities, and the railway systems which are equipping Russia and China have been financed by Belgian stock companies.

The organization of credit is also a part of the mechanism of competition in which economy, flexibility, and the highest efficiency are important elements. The nation which maintains a currency that is needlessly expensive hampers every part of the machinery of production and exchange. A high rental for currency and for the use of capital imposes needless charges upon the conduct of all enterprises. Enterprises which might have paid a reasonable profit under a lower money rate cease to pay such a profit and may be driven to the wall by foreign competitors.

This stifling of production, by the lack of the tools of exchange or an excessive price for them, may throw its pall over whole communities, as is the case in the South to-day, from the absence of an elastic banking currency. It is obvious that the absence of any such thing as money would greatly hamper the exchange of products, cripple production, diminish the means for employing labor and the demand for it, and hopelessly handicap the nation in such a position. It should be equally obvious, with a little thought, that an insufficiency of the tools of exchange would cause the same embarrassments in somewhat less degree. It is not additional quantities of "primary money" that are needed in industrial communities, but simply such an organization of the system of credit as shall afford an adequate equipment of credit money at the times when it is needed for special purposes, without any other restrictions than such as are necessary to insure uniformity and safety. From this point of view, greater freedom of banking issues, within the limits of safety, may be as vital for keeping labor employed to its maximum capacity as for affording an indispensable tool to the capitalist.

One of the remarkable phases of modern capitalism is the development of nations whose preëminent functions seem to be those of lenders, bankers, and carriers. The position which they occupy in the scheme of international trade has become so radically different from that of the borrowing nations that the entire theory of "the balance of trade," as once understood, has been upset. Great Britain, the most conspicuous of the lending nations, shows annually an excess of imports of merchandise over exports, approaching a thousand millions of dollars, and this balance is far from rectified by the movement of the precious metals. This condition, according to the old mercantile theories, should have denuded England of her gold and driven her people into bankruptcy. That nothing of the kind has occurred is not an impeachment of these theories under all conditions, but simply a proof that conditions have arisen to which they are no longer applicable.

Great Britain for many years sent her surplus products abroad, without receiving payment in anything but engraved pieces of paper representing government bonds and corporate securities. The loan which she then made, trusting to the future for its repayment, is coming back in a shower of the world's riches, in payment of the interest upon the capital she advanced to her colonies and other struggling young peoples. To-day, while some of her writers bemoan her agricultural and manufacturing decline, she continues to grow rich by her three functions of lender, banker, and carrier.

Whether a nation can safely substitute these intermediary functions for independent production may be a subject for reasonable debate. The process may be carried too far, and may produce a stationary condition of industry and invention which will finally relegate the capitalistic nations to the rear in the competition with the poorer industrial nations, just as the great capitalist may cease to exercise the energy and thought which were necessary to his earlier achievements, and enabled him finally to distance his older rivals. But for many years, at least, the capitalistic nations, with a large fund of surplus capital loaned abroad, will occupy a commanding position in the world's finance.

It is by a natural evolution of events that they have become bankers, brokers, merchants, and carriers for other peoples. The nation, like the individual, as already pointed out, first provides for its most pressing needs, and in marketing its raw materials and surplus products avails itself of the capital and carrying resources of other peoples. It is only when capital becomes redundant that competition can be carried on upon equal terms with those who are content with a low return upon it. Under this disadvantage of scarcity of capital and high rates for it, the United States long labored in their effort to build up a carrying and banking trade outside of their own limits in competition with nations content with a low return upon their saved capital. Whether great political and economic ends will be served by levying taxes upon the community to create a merchant marine may be a subject for debate, but even the demand for such action is not likely to be seriously made until the surplus of capital and low rates for money are upon the eve of bringing the natural equipment of the country up to the point where such investments might profitably be made out of private savings.

The average judgment of the unlearned, directed by the instinct of self-interest, is sometimes wiser than the reasoning that clings to abstract dogmas without regard to changes in conditions. It has been the fashion for many years to rail at the supporters of the mercantile theory as though they were the most unreasoning and foolish of men. The mercantilists did, in fact, put the cart before the horse, to a large degree, by treating as a cause of prosperity what was in reality only its symbol. They saw that the communities that accumulated gold were those which were the most prosperous. Instead of reasoning, therefore, that prosperity should be invoked in order to attract gold, they sometimes appeared to reason as though every effort should be made to obtain gold, upon the theory that prosperity would be dragged at the chariot wheels of the yellow metal. It is doubtful if the more intelligent supporters of the theory took so crude a view, even if they failed to grasp all the bearings of the problem. The element of soundness in their position, which is generally ignored by modern economists, lies in the fact that the precious metals are the most exchangeable of commodities. It is this that has led to their selection by a process of evolution, and not by mere convention, as the material for money.

Under the modern system, with the laws

extending over nearly every land the protection of the sanctity of contracts and permitting a steady current of industry and wealth through the various forms of raw material, labor, and finished product, gold seems to have become almost the least important thing in the elaborate mechanism of economic life. But at a time when contracts could be violated with impunity, when production was arrested by wars and by the interference of official tyranny, when persecution drove the Jew, the Protestant, or the Catholic in turn into exile, there was a preëminent quality in the possession of gold which justified the preference for it shown by individuals and communities. It was the one form of wealth that could be readily transported, that could be securely hidden in small compass without injury by rust or time, and which never lost the characteristic of the highest form of value, in spite of fluctuations in its purchasing power. The holder of gold saw his wealth appreciating when other things were depreciating, and if it depreciated when other things were rising in price, the fact was concealed by the feeling of abounding prosperity which reigned in industry.

The lesson that changed conditions give a new aspect to economic problems, even though they do not falsify old laws, cannot be ignored in the period of economic revolution through which the world is passing. The doctrines of *laissez faire*, consecrated as they are by their association with the emancipation of industry from mediæval fetters, must be adapted to modern conditions. They will never lose their value as the fundamental principles of political economy, but the time has passed when the functions of the state can be limited to those which were thought sufficient in the infancy of industry.

The real problem for every modern state that hopes to compete for supremacy in the world's markets is the old one of so adjusting every part of the mechanism of its industrial and moral life as to obtain the greatest results from the smallest expenditure of labor. The classical political economy declared that this result was best attained by leaving free play to every individual will and genius in the struggle for existence. Within certain limits this great principle can never be impeached. It is the underlying principle of all economic life. But the principle of association and coöperation also has a place in political economy, and a place which has grown larger as the family has been absorbed into the tribe, the tribe into the nation, and the nation into the industrial empire.

This principle of association declares that there are some things which can be better done by union among men than by the man acting alone. The modern tendency is toward the specialization of talent, — the assignment to one man of the work for which he is best fitted. The community in which this specialization is most perfect will produce the largest results with the least effort. Consolidation in politics and industry contributes to this end by concentrating work enough of a special class for one man or group of men to do, instead of leaving each to perform indifferently a variety of functions. In the most primitive community, if distribution and credit could be organized, better results would be obtained if one set of men devoted all their time to fishing, others to hunting, and others to boat-building, than if each worked indifferently at all these vocations. If this is true under primitive conditions, it is infinitely more important under the severe conditions of modern competition.

This necessity for specialization and consolidation, in order to equip a people for successful competition in the markets of the world, is the explanation of many of the tendencies of the last few years. The importance of reducing competing production to its most efficient basis is the reason for the consolidation of industries, the growth of trusts, the abolition of middlemen, and for appeals to the state to clear the path of production and exchange of every needless obstacle. Larger freight cars, heavier locomotives, freight tariffs which discriminate neither against individuals, classes of goods, nor communities; public docks and harbors deep enough for the largest and most economical transports, with adequate lighting and safeguarding of the coasts, reducing losses and the cost of marine insurance; the adoption of a single monetary standard and the proper organization of credit; innumerable measures to protect and make definite business contracts, — all these are only steps in this process of complete industrial equipment.

Even those expenditures by the state which seem to have the character of luxuries serve the same controlling purpose, when they do not impose undue burdens upon production. Technical schools, works of art which serve as the constant model for skill and beauty in industrial work, and even the higher education which gives breadth of view, keenness of insight, and accuracy of judgment, may all contribute toward the creation and perpetuation of a producing and industrial state whose competition will be irresistible in the struggle for commercial supremacy.

VI

THE UNITED STATES AS A WORLD POWER — NATURE OF THE ECONOMIC AND POLITICAL PROBLEM

THE appearance of the United States in the circle of world powers having possessions in the Orient, although seemingly sudden and unexpected, has been a natural evolution of recent political and economic tendencies. The time has come when the intensity of the struggle for new markets and for opportunities for investment has forced the great commercial nations, by the instinct of self-preservation, to demand that the field of competition be kept open, even by the exercise, if necessary, of paramount military force. In supporting this demand the United States will obey the motive of enlightened self-interest which actuates other producing nations. She cannot take any other course without condemning herself to industrial stagnation at home as well as to a loss in prestige abroad. The appearance of foreign states as borrowers in the New York money market is one of the many signs that the period of economic isolation for the United States is drawing to an end, and that she must enter into the competition for the world market and into the field of international finance.

In this contest the problem for the United States, on the economic side, is to attain the greatest producing capacity by the efficiency of competitive machinery and labor, while on the political side it is to keep open the opportunity for the free play of this competitive power in the world's markets. If commercial freedom were the rule among nations, so that there could be no discrimination against the most efficient producer, the industries of the United States would need no political support in the contest for commercial supremacy. But, by reason of the conditions which have prevailed in the world from the beginning, under which diplomatic finesse and military force have been brought to the support of national commerce, it is essential that those peoples who can produce under the best conditions should not be deprived of the opportunity to sell in the world's markets. This is the significance of the economic and political problem which confronts the American people, and which makes important their foothold in the Philippines as a lever for keeping open the door of China and for sharing in the development of Asia.

Let us examine a little more closely the nature of the contest which confronts modern producing nations, and discover, if possible, the best way for winning and holding supremacy in that contest.

The controlling element of the economic problem is the greatly increased severity of competition. This is due to a combination of the factors which make up the complex conditions of modern industrial life. Among these factors are the division of labor, the development of machinery, the growth of capital, and the revolution in the means of transportation. The mere appearance of the locomotive and the ocean steamship as factors in production and exchange, while producing a remarkable revolution, did not at once level the barriers between markets. Freight rates were much higher a generation or a score of years ago than they are at present; and it required their gradual reduction to the minimum cost of the service rendered to bring into play the full efficiency of railways and canals in merging isolated local markets into a world market, sensitive to every flash of the electric wire bringing the news of a crop failure, a cabinet decision, an act of Congress, or the declaration of a railway dividend in the most distant quarter of the globe. It required also the adaptation of industry to the new conditions before producers could begin to reach out beyond their own country.

As Professor Liesse declares, in his original and striking book, "Le Travail aux Points de Vue Scientifique, Industriel, et Social," "The concentration of industries has been accompanied by a more and more extended expansion of markets. To local competition were added first that of the surrounding region and then that of the entire country. Finally, in spite of economic fetters, competition has become international." It is upon this international competition that the United States are compelled to enter, whether they wish it or not, by the conditions of their industrial development. Their production of finished goods and their fund of saved capital have overrun the needs of the home market. But in seeking to enter the world market this country finds rivals seeking to fence off particular portions for themselves, and to frame the rules of the contest in such manner as to take away the element of a fair fight under the conditions of economic freedom. How a continent has been thus fenced off is well set forth by Professor Schurman, President of Cornell University, in his speech on "Expansion," before the Union League Club of Chicago, on February 22, 1900: —

> "In our blind idolatry of the Monroe doctrine, in our devotion to the stay-at-home policy of the eighteenth century, in our intense desire to avoid all international obligations, we have allowed great nations of Europe to partition out Africa among themselves and exclude American products by means of discriminating tariffs devised to secure for their own manufacturers a monopoly of the new markets."

The conditions which confront the business world to-day are essentially the product of very recent years. Cheapness and swiftness of transportation removed one of the insuperable barriers to the creation of a world market, but they did not in themselves create it. At least three other steps were required — the organization of industry, the growth of a fund of capital sufficient for production upon a large scale, and the development of organized markets. It is because these are approaching the goal of an organized world market that the conditions of competition between different peoples have suddenly become so acute that diplomacy and the sword are being invoked, on the one side to secure exclusive opportunities, and on the other to preserve equality of conditions. So long as the American producer limited his activity to the home market, and a complacent government lent him the aid of a high tariff to put his experiments on a firm footing as well as to shut out sporadic competition after these experiments had become established industries, it mattered little to him that Tunis or Madagascar had closed their doors to any trade but that of France, or that Russia was gaining financial control of Persia, and was trying to shut her rivals out of Turkey and to dictate the trade policy of China. But within a few years the eyes of the American manufacturer have been suddenly opened to the fact that there is a world market in which he must be a competitor if he would dispose of his products and find labor for the thousands expecting it at his hands, and that equal opportunities in this market can be preserved only by the resolute support of his government.

If the problem were a purely economic one, it could be solved upon purely economic grounds. Under this head alone, however, there is much that is novel in the severity of competition. It is evident that every factor which affects cost of production and transportation will affect competitive power. Such diverse things as the size of cars and locomotives, the rates for the loaning of money, the efficiency of the currency, the prizes offered for the invention of labor-saving machinery, the freedom of transactions from needless restrictions and taxes, and the burden falling upon industry for the maintenance of the state and the army, will all be elements in determining the cost and efficiency of production in any community in competition with its rivals.

Transportation is one of those sciences in which economy and efficiency mean much in the acuteness of modern competition. The American railway system is superior to that of European countries already in the size of locomotives and of cars, and in cost of service. As a rule, European distances are so slight that economy in car-space, power, and freight rates has not yet become a controlling factor in the competition with America; but every reduction in the cost of moving freight over the great distances in the United States increases the competing power of this country. Professor Henry T. Newcomb, whose researches have shed so much light upon railway development, showed, in a report to the Department of Agriculture in 1898, that the average revenue from freight per ton per mile on the railways of the United States fell from 1.613 cents in 1873 to 0.806 cents in 1896, a decline of 50 per cent. in twenty-three years.

Nearly every year has contributed some new element to this reduction of the cost of transportation. Steel rails have supplanted iron, train-brakes have reduced the cost and increased the safety of handling trains, and (to quote from Professor Newcomb) "the general use of larger locomotives has led to a considerable increase in the average number of cars in each train, which has been accompanied by a notable tendency to substitute larger cars for those which, in the natural course of business, have to be replaced, thus increasing very materially the efficiency of the train as a machine for moving commodities."

The development of organized industry upon a large scale was a necessary prerequisite to competition in a world market. The division of labor, the use of expensive special machinery capable of producing goods far beyond the requirements of local markets, and reduced cost of superintendence, are among the elements in this organization of industry. The removal of the barriers of distance paved the way for production upon a large scale, and for the development of these economies to the highest degree. It became possible for each industry to find a home, without regard to distance from its markets, in the community affording the best conditions for production — manufactures of iron near the mines, and manufactures of textiles in the towns and cities where an organized body of skillful workers already existed. It became possible not only to transport materials greater distances from the place of their origin to the place where they were to be made up, but also to distribute finished products with greater economy at long distances from the original place of manufacture.

This specialization of industry was not accomplished in a day. The railway development of the world hardly attained serious proportions before 1870, and was far from complete within the memory of men still in their prime. Professor Newcomb, in his work on "Railway Economics," calls attention to the fact that in the United States "more than half of the present railway mileage has been constructed since 1880." In 1870 this mileage was only 49,160. There was an increase of 70 per cent. to 1880; but even at that date the railways of the United States had a length of only 87,724 miles, which was destined to rise by 1890 to 163,597 miles. The growth since then has been less rapid, because the equipment of the country has been approaching completion.

In France, the growth in railways in operation, exclusive of local lines and tramways, rose from 17,221 kilometres in 1872, to 37,739 kilometres in 1900. In Russia, within the short period from 1887 to 1900, according to the "Russian Journal of Financial Statistics" for January, the mileage of the state railways has risen from 2,928 to 20,346 miles. In the whole of Europe, according to an article by Professor Edmond Théry in "l'Economiste Européen" of January 5, 1900, the aggregate of railways in operation increased from 134,591 kilometres on January 1, 1875, to 269,743 kilometres (165,000 miles) by December 31, 1898. When the very recent character of this development is weighed for a moment, it becomes clear that the nations of the civilized world are only standing upon the threshold of the world market, and that the struggle for its possession is yet before them.

The development of industries upon a scale for supplying this world market necessarily followed at some remove the organization of the means of transportation. This organization reduced to a minimum the friction involved in bringing products into the world market. It remained to take advantage of these conditions by increasing the supply as the market widened and the demand increased. How remarkable a development has been witnessed in this direction within one or two decades was set forth in an address delivered at Chicago, on February 20, by Secretary Gage. He pointed out that, while from 1870 to 1899, population in the United States increased by 100 per cent., exports increased from $392,771,768 to $1,227,023,302, or 212 per cent.; production of wheat rose from 235,884,700 to 547,303,843 bushels, or 132 per cent.; pig iron, from 1,665,179 to 11,773,934 tons, or 607 per cent.; steel produced, from 68,750 to 8,932,857 tons, or more than twelve thousand per cent.; telegraphic messages, from 9,157,646 to 76,805,175 in number, or 739 per cent.; post-office receipts, from $19,772,221 to $95,021,384, or 380 per cent.; and salaries paid in public schools, from $37,832,556 to $123,809,412, or 227 per cent.

The last item is one among many which are specially significant of the changed conditions of modern life, because they illustrate how large a surplus fund is left for the employment of the professional classes and for ministration to higher ideals after full provision has been made for the exacting conditions of the struggle for existence. It is out of this great surplus that large professional salaries and growing taxes for public improvements are paid, with great benefits both to the competing power and to the higher life of a community, while leaving larger resources than a generation ago for the necessaries and comforts of the working people.

The accumulation of capital is another modern fact contributing greatly to the concentration of industry, by permitting a greater and greater division of labor, resulting in the growing efficiency of the individual at his special task and a greater aggregate product from a given number of workers. The growth of the fund of surplus capital has made possible investments in machinery and manufacturing plants which would not have been conceivable a few generations ago. It has been possible to make investments in enterprises requiring a long time for their completion, like transcontinental railways, interoceanic canals, and tunnels, for which the world could not have afforded to spare the capital when its resources were comparatively limited.

When the French railway system was inaugurated, in 1860, it required — in spite of the great progress which had been made in the use of machinery and the saving of capital — the intervention of the Bank of France to sustain the necessary financial operations and obtain from the public sufficient subscriptions of capital for carrying on the work. The amount of capital called for in any single year was not more than $60,000,000, which would be treated as a moderate single transaction in the financial operations of to-day. Regarding the total capital of about $2,700,000,000, representing the value of the French railway system at the present time, Professor Liesse declares that "even the boldest spirits would have been astonished about the middle of the century if the possibility could have been revealed to them of assembling all this capital for a special object, without exhausting the available resources demanded by all the other branches of progressive industry." But now every year witnesses nearly as large an offer as this of savings for the use of industry. The compilation of the new securities issued in the civilized world made up annually by the

"Moniteur des Intérêts Matériels," the well-known Belgian financial journal, shows the amount to have been 9,129,054,150 francs in 1896, 8,911,870,530 francs in 1897, 8,902,776,660 francs in 1898, and 10,577,-406,550 francs in 1899. The issues of railway and industrial securities alone in 1898 were 5,448,091,660 francs, and in 1899, 6,648,483,960 francs, or more than twenty times the amount needed in France in 1860 to inaugurate the railway system of the country.

The manner in which the great fund of savings, groping for safe investment, is piling up in civilized countries is indicated by a glance at the increase in deposits in the European savings systems. Let us take a few illustrations at random: The Prussian savings banks increased their deposits within the five years ending with 1898 by about 40 per cent., or by a sum of more than $350,-000,000. The French private savings banks at the close of 1899 carried deposits of 3,405,647,025 francs ($657,000,000), equal to about $16 for each inhabitant of France. The impoverished people of Italy, sinking under the burdens of an excessive military establishment and a foreign policy too ambitious for the resources of the country, showed deposits in the ordinary and postal savings banks at the close of 1899 amounting to nearly $400,000,000. The savings of Belgium deposited in the savings banks run much above $100,000,000. Even in Russia, which is suffering under industrial depression and serious famines, the savings deposits in different classes of banks rose from 518,537,000 roubles on November 30, 1898, to 580,331,000 roubles ($308,500,000) by September 30, 1899. In the United States the growth of deposits in the savings banks was from $549,874,358 in 1870 to $2,230,366,954 in 1899.

So rapidly has this accumulation of money affected interest rates, by creating a supply of capital in excess of the demand, that conversion of debts at a lower rate of interest was one of the most striking features of the money market and the stock exchanges prior to 1897. There was a hardening of discount rates in the latter year, resulting from the opening of new outlets for investment, including the new industrial activity in the undeveloped countries of Africa and the East.

This supply of surplus capital has resulted in the creation of great banking institutions, handling a speculative fund of thousands of millions of dollars, which often plays a dangerous part in the stock market when it is not loaned in the ordinary operations of production. This great fund shifts from market to market under the impulse of slight differences in the discount rate or the rental for gold; sometimes threatening as much damage to the small investor, who counts upon steady values, as a cannon-ball let loose upon the deck of a rolling ship. The ability to draw upon this fund at moderate rates has, however, permitted the constant growth of the concentration of industry, and this concentration has permitted great economies in methods of production. Towns and cities have sprung up at the waving of the magic wand of organized capital, and the creation of varied industries on a grand scale has brought about the birth of various related industries.

An important phase of the movement of capital is its international character. In his interesting book, "The Evolution of Modern Capitalism," Mr. Hobson truthfully declares that "dealers in stock exchange securities and in the precious metals are in active, constant competition at all the great commercial centres of the world." International finance has become a power which disregards boundaries, takes scant account of personal and class feelings, and sometimes dictates terms to nations. In its ordinary functions, however, its work is beneficent. It governs the equations between values in different markets by sending capital to those markets where its rental is highest and, therefore, where its efficiency is greatest in ministering to the needs of the race. The free movement of capital between international markets, selfish and pitiless as it seems to be, is in reality but the fluctuation of the barometer of need and supply, the application of the law of greatest usefulness to the most sensitive and responsive of the tools of modern social development.

It is not a matter of surprise, therefore, but rather a natural result of this increase of competition, that industry should attempt to throw up barriers for its own protection. While competition was local, the producer of moderate capacity could hold a local market by the fixed customs of his clientage, and by the difficulty of bringing products from a distance into competition with his. He may have made mistakes in buying raw material, and in employing out-of-date and wasteful means of manufacture; but if he had no local competitors, or if they all pursued the same indolent and inefficient methods, he had nothing to fear from competitors from without.

Cheapness and rapidity of transportation by land and water changed all this. Within the limits where freight charges did not eat up economies of production, the most ingenious and up-to-date producer was enabled to find the spots in the world where production was less efficiently organized than his own, and to drive the local producer there to the wall. As these limits set by the cost of carriage became more and more widely extended, it came to be seen that the only defense against such competition was for the weaker concerns to surrender to the stronger, or to secure an agreement by which there should be a voluntary abstention of the one from entering the territory of the other, or a division of profits or business. Thus the extent and intensity of competition due to the widening of markets forced producers to turn to pools, combinations, and trusts as a natural weapon of self-defense. The great corporation, possessing the most efficient machinery, naturally supersedes the mere pool or trust, and contributes much more to the competing power of the community.

It is when the "trust" has swallowed up its rivals for the control of the local market, and reaches out for the control of foreign markets, that it seeks to bring political power to the aid of economic efficiency or inefficiency, and thus projects the problem of controlling the international market into the field of world politics. It is this struggle between the great political powers of the world for bolstering up national economic power which constitutes the cardinal fact of modern diplomacy. The issue involved is sometimes obscured by motives which seem to be purely national and political, rather than economic; but the controlling fact is coming home more and more to statesmen, even of the least advanced countries, that the real basis of national power is capacity for competitive production. Henceforth, therefore, the aim of national leaders promises more and more to become the finding and keeping of markets and fields for investment — in fine, the creation of national trusts vested with the power of taxation and with military and naval force for the object of seeking and holding exclusive markets on the one hand, and of increasing national competing power in free markets on the other.

That this conception of the great state trust, fusing into one mighty combination for distinctly economic ends all the industrial and military power of a nation, is no figment of the imagination, is plainly demonstrated by recent events. Conditions in Asia, Africa, and South America bear witness to its reality. As Senator Depew, of New York, so forcibly remarked, in a recent speech: —

"To relieve home congestion, starvation, and revolution, England, Germany, and France are increasing their armies, enlarging their fleets, and either waging war or on the eve of great conflicts, while partitioning Africa, threatening China, seizing Asiatic principalities, and madly building railroads across the continents of Asia and Africa. By victorious war and triumphant diplomacy we are in our own territory within easy reach, at Manila, of China, Siam, Korea, Annam, the

East Indies, and Japan. Without war or entangling alliances we will have equal rights with other nations to the ports of the Orient, with all that it means for the demonstrated superiority of our manufactures and the surplus harvests of our farms."

The keenness of international competition for trade is illustrated not only by the actual colonial establishments of the great powers, but by the appointment of special commissions to investigate trade conditions abroad, and by the effort to raise the consular service to the highest degree of efficiency. Great Britain has sent two special commissions to China recently to investigate the opportunities for trade there, and Lord Charles Beresford has interested the world in the proposition that this great market should be kept open to free competition. The French government has sent two commissions of merchant experts to China, who have made reports of great value, which are kept under the seal of secrecy for the benefit of French trade. The German government has taken similar steps to open trade opportunities, and sustains by its political prestige investments of German capital in banks and railways in South America and Turkey.

The new German railway in the province of Shantung is not only supported by a syndicate of the strongest German banks, including the Disconto Gesellschaft, but, according to the "Moniteur des Intérêts Matériels" of December 3, 1899, is under the direct protection of the German Foreign Office, and will share its earnings with the imperial government. The German Empire, moreover, through control of the railway system at home, offers a system of differential rates to her exporters, in order to enable them to increase their sales of German products in foreign markets. The United States are awakening to the necessity of organizing their consular service upon the basis of merit; and even Sweden, according to a recent consular report, has appointed a special commission to ascertain in what manner Swedish consuls can best further the export trade of the country.

But, perhaps, the most perfect example of the great state trust bringing to the aid of national competing power all the resources of military and political force is that of the empire of Russia. On this point it is only necessary to quote the language of a semi-official Russian publication, just issued for the first time in English, "The Russian Journal of Financial Statistics." Here is its definition of the economic position of the Russian state:—

"Russia, as a nation and a country, is far behind England in wealth, and America in productiveness. In regard to accumulated wealth, it is behind other countries as well, viz., France and Germany. But this does not prevent the Russian *state* from being by far *the greatest economic unit on the face of the globe.* It is true, of course, that its national debt, almost equal to that of England, is far less than the national debt of France, while its railway-net is neither as extensive nor as valuable as Germany's. But, on the other hand, if one turns to its assets, it will be seen that the Russian state occupies a unique position. As a landowner, it draws an annual *net profit* of 45 million roubles from its forests, mines, and agricultural property; the land it has ceded to or purchased for the communities of ex-serfs bring it in over 800 million roubles; as a constructor and purchaser of railways, it is building one of the longest lines in the world, and works 20,300 miles of railway on its own account, the *net* profit on which, $68,000,000, represents one seventh of that on all the railways of the United States. Besides being a capitalist and banker, the Russian state is a metallurgist and spirit merchant. Apart from its banking operations, the State Treasury in 1898 received over $850,000,000 into its safes, nearly 400 millions of which had nothing in common with revenue from taxation. What private person, what family, however fabulously rich it may be; what railway company, however extensive its railway-net; what trust, can show figures like these? Even the budget of such a country as France is outstripped by $200,000,000."[1]

The Russian Empire, therefore, may be described as the greatest "trust" in the world. From the natural attributes of government monopoly it meets no opposition on Russian soil. Seeking to guard industry at home by high tariffs, and to promote competition abroad by distributing with a generous hand in loans and bounties the gold derived from the infinite resources of international finance, and armed with absolute command over many millions of people, who are accustomed to ready submission to the military system, the Russian Empire represents the greatest organized force which confronts Western civilization. "Upon the highlands of Central Asia," as Professor Williams so tersely declared in a brilliant address before the American Academy of Political and Social Science, in April, 1899,

[1] This extract is printed just as it appears in the Russian publication in English, except that sums in English pounds sterling are converted into American money.

"have been bred in the past the races which overran and dominated the civilized West; and where these swarms were once raised other millions may spring up in the future to obey the call of the conqueror and spread devastation among those more cultured but less lusty peoples who represent our race."

Russian policy proceeds without interruption along the lines of least resistance, but with many resources for removing obstacles where they are encountered. This policy is directed by an educated and far-sighted autocracy, who keep steadily before them the end of making Russia the ruler of Europe and Asia. While smooth words drop from the lips of Russian ambassadors at foreign courts, the Council of Ministers at St. Petersburg, with its diplomatic and financial agents scheming in Central Asia, watches for new opportunities for extending Russian influence. Professor Williams, in the article already quoted, written more than a year ago, declared — with a prescience which would have been wonderful but for the known continuity of Russian policy — that, "though for the time being there is little advertisement of Russian Asia in the newspapers, it is not likely that she has abandoned her earlier intention of securing Turkey. Even Persia and India remain well within the horizon of her ambition." These predictions have been verified by the creation of a Russian bank at the capital of Persia, which has advanced about $12,000,000 to pay off the debts of the empire, upon the condition that the custom-house receipts shall be pledged for the payment of interest on the loan. As the London "Statist" of February 3, 1900, well remarks: "The Loan Bank, which is in reality a Russian state concern, will obtain complete control over the custom-houses of Persia, if the interest falls in arrear, and unless the whole government of Persia is reformed, it is perfectly certain that the interest will fall in arrear." Obviously, remarks the English journal, "the Russian government has been quick in availing itself of our troubles in South Africa, for it is hardly likely that our Foreign Office would look on approvingly while these negotiations were being conducted, if it were not already too much occupied with more pressing matters."

Intrenched in Central Asia, Russia, with

her railway system completed, would be in a strategic position which would endanger not only all China, but also the English possessions in India. The Chinese-Eastern railway, the eastern branch of the trans-Siberian, cuts directly across the Chinese province of Manchuria to Port Arthur, which has been already leased by the decrepit Chinese government to the Russian Empire. Offshoots from this railway, as it skirts the southern border of Asiatic Russia, will give Russia the ability to mass troops at any point along the British frontier, and to draw upon the millions of hardy cavalry of the great steppes, almost in the twinkling of an eye, while Great Britain is moving troops and supplies by the circuitous water route through the Mediterranean, the Suez canal, and the ports of India.

The scope of Russian plans does not stop with the completion of the trans-Siberian line. Already engineers are studying the preferable route for the trans-Caspian railway, which will lead direct from the boundary of European and Asiatic Russia through the heart of Persia, giving Russia a port on the Persian Gulf, and enabling her to flank

British India on the west. Only in the case of the Bagdad railway, which will be an extension of the German lines in Asiatic Turkey, does Russia seem to have been outgeneraled by another power hungry for world empire and the opportunities for financial exploitation. How far-reaching and well advanced are Russian plans for bringing Western Asia under her political and economic system is set forth in a striking manner by Mr. Alexander Hume Ford in "The Century" for March, 1900. He says: —

"This situation has been foreseen by Russia for at least a generation. Like a hand, the palm of which firmly covers Siberia and Transcaspia, the Czar has planted his railway system in Asia. From this strong palm five fingers radiate, and feel their way preparatory to closing in for the next firm grasp. At present an apparently weak and insignificant finger of steel is gradually slipping from its point of connection with the palm, in the Caucasus, towards Constantinople; it has made some progress. The next finger almost touches Teheran, and is gliding down through Persia to the gulf. The middle finger slips out from under the palm at Merv, in Central Asia; it has touched Herat, and, unless stopped, will soon reach Kandahar and the Arabian Sea, touching British India teasingly in the ribs near Karachi. The index-finger, starting from Samarkand, has already reached the border of China."

It is obvious that with the completion of this railway system Russia would be in a position, in case of war, to dominate Asia. Massing her forces round the Caspian Sea, and pouring reinforcements at short range and by quick railway runs upon any threatened point, she would be able to imitate the effective tactics of Napoleon's early campaigns, striking from a secure centre at the weakest points on the scattered lines of her enemies.

When to this remarkable military position is added the power which a nation organized like Russia derives from the resources of international finance, some conception may be formed of the economic and political engine which is being perfected at St. Petersburg. Finance, by the issue of negotiable securities, and by the shifting of these securities from one national market to another under the attraction of trifling differences in price and in the discount rates, has come to recognize no national boundaries or local obligations. Among the most conspicuous of the so-called "international securities" are the government loans and the guaranteed railway bonds of the Russian Empire. So skillfully has Russia appealed to investors, and so steadily has she built up her international credit, that, within the thirteen years from 1887 to 1900, as set forth in "l'Economiste Européen" of January 26, 1900, she has increased the nominal capital of her debt by more than 40 per cent., — from 11,619,432,000 francs to 16,453,691,000 francs ($3,200,000,000), — while the annual debt charge, including some contributions towards the sinking fund, actually fell from 278,591,000 roubles to 274,612,000 roubles ($140,000,000). The meaning of these figures is that the Russian Empire has obtained from the investing community — and nearly all of it from the savings of Western civilization — the use of about a thousand millions of dollars for equipping her railway system, creating a navy, and strengthening her internal resources, and this without adding a penny to the amount which she was already paying for the use of a little more than two thousand millions.

It is into the deep well of the world's investment fund that Russia has been able to dip almost without stint for carrying out her imperial plans since she began to show her ostentatious friendship for France, and since she anchored her credit to a firm foundation by adopting the gold standard. It was the avowed purpose of M. de Witte, the resourceful minister of finance, who has risen from a railway employee at a flag-station to one of the most powerful places in the world, to attract foreign capital into Russia by putting an end to the régime of paper money and adopting the gold standard.

Within three or four years, without having to wait to educate public opinion or to combat the fallacies of popular agitators, decree after decree was issued which raised Russian paper money to a fixed rate of exchange, authorized gold contracts, accumulated the largest gold store in the world, and permitted the resumption of gold payments on demand. Within the three years from October 1, 1896, to October 1, 1899, the paper money in circulation fell from 1,047,600,000 roubles ($545,000,000) to 555,000,000 roubles ($290,000,000), fully covered by gold; and the gold in circulation rose from 30,300,000 roubles ($16,000,000) to 662,300,000 roubles ($345,000,000). Never perhaps in the history of the world was a calculated cause, where so many diverse elements were involved, followed so promptly by the expected result. Foreign capital poured into Russia in a stream of gold and goods which equipped mines and mills and factories with the resources of production; and within four years more joint stock companies were floated than had been formed in a century before.

If military and industrial rivals are not to be fed upon the great savings fund of Western civilization, this fund must find employment for itself, and give employment to labor in fields where its use will contribute to the ethical as well as the industrial progress of the world. If all markets were open, if all opportunities for labor and for employing the fruits of labor were free to men of all nations upon equal terms, that nation would confess its cowardice and decadence which was not willing to trust its fate on the economic field to the energy, inventive genius, and productive power of its people. It is precisely because certain states seem to fear this competition, and desire not only to deprive it of all conditions of equality, but to exclude its influence completely from undeveloped countries, that intervention is justified by those states which represent in the truest sense the political and social ideals of Western civilization. To them is intrusted the solution of the economic problem by the demand on their part for a fair field for its working out, in which all peoples shall have an equal opportunity. Toward this great end the American people can afford to devote their most strenuous efforts, serene in the faith that under such conditions their own victory will be sure, and that they will serve the highest interests of civilization.

VII

THE UNITED STATES AS A WORLD POWER — THEIR ADVANTAGES IN THE COMPETITION FOR COMMERCIAL EMPIRE

Having defined the nature of the economic problem which confronts the nations in the struggle for commercial empire, it remains to consider the means for winning supremacy in this struggle and the advantages and disadvantages under which the United States enter the contest. The fact that the shutting up of markets, diplomatic intrigue, and even the sword are factors in the contest takes it beyond the purely economic field and sets it on a stage where the play of the great forces of passion, patriotism, and race conflict give surpassing interest to the drama of world history.

We have seen that intensity of competition in a world-wide market is the dominating note of modern industrial life. We have seen that the highest efficiency of every factor in production is the only means of winning in the economic field, but that states which fear to trust their forces in this field may throw the sword into the balance, as Brennus tossed his blade upon the scales which weighed the gold to ransom Rome. It behooves the nation, therefore, which would succeed in the economic contest to be prepared also for the final test of force, which has not ceased to be a factor in the world's affairs. In dealing with the position of the United States in this contest, it will appear that they enjoy many advantages inherent in the character of the race and the development of republican institutions, but that the very breadth of these advantages involves some impairment of the unity and force which belong to absolutism.

The question of the relative efficiency of the United States and their industrial rivals involves the factors of political organization, natural resources, economic power, and social development. Among the elements which reach into both the political and economic field is the modern tendency towards concentration. The old maxim, "In union there is strength," is receiving a new meaning by the movement towards great empires in the political field and business consolidations in the economic field. The secret of Russia's present power is not the wealth of any single part of her domain, but the vast extent of the territory over which it reaches, drawing race after race in Central Asia under the empire of the "Great White Czar," and inspiring something of the feeling which Mr. Bryce says prevailed in the ancient world, "that as the dominion of Rome was universal, so it must be eternal." In any contest in diplomacy or in the field, the consolidated empire is likely to prevail over a loose alliance of smaller rivals, because of its ability to strike heavily and quickly by consulting only a single controlling head. In the field of industry also the people which can draw upon a wide field at home for its raw materials, and distribute them over a wide domestic market, without encountering the barriers of customs tariffs and differences in the organization of industry, will prevail over competitors whose narrow limits deprive them of the economies which come from concentration.

The United States enter upon the conflict for world empire enjoying a great advantage over the democracies of antiquity and over the smaller nations of Western Europe. The extent of the domain of the republic, embracing half a continent under a uniform policy of laws and commerce, is an important advantage at the outset of this contest. The movement towards concentration of political power and the elimination of small governments has been advancing with rapid strides during the last two centuries. In the United States, the sovereign power of the States has been steadily yielding to the demand of the people that uniformity shall prevail throughout the territory of the Union. In Western Europe, the partition of Poland, the union of Austria and Hungary, the realization of Italian unity, the creation of the German Empire under the headship of Prussia, are all symptoms of the centripetal movement which has extended from politics to industry. Professor Williams, of Yale University, in his address at the annual meeting of the American Academy of Political and Social Science a year ago, asked this question: —

"Have we any assurance that we have reached the end of a readjustment that has eliminated the names of Burgundy, of Savoy, and of Poland from the map of Europe, or that such existing survivals as Belgium, or Denmark, or Bulgaria are not destined sooner or later to follow in their train?"

He might have added that already this principle was receiving application in the British occupation of Egypt, the absorption of Algeria and Tunis by France, and the financial control of the powers in Greece. And within a year after he wrote, hints of German dominance in Holland, continued encroachments on the local rights of Finland, and the growth of the financial influence of Great Britain in Portugal afforded new illustrations of this world tendency.

The United States, therefore, are following the same process of absorbing adjacent territory which began with the organization of the Northwestern territory, the purchase of Louisiana, the acquisition of Florida from its Spanish masters, the absorption of the republic of Texas, and the conquest of California, and brought the expulsion of Spain from Cuba and Porto Rico. While Russia advances with giant strides in Central Asia, the great republic of the West is pursuing the same inevitable destiny, and tending to put herself upon an equal plane for the contest which

Professor Williams so strikingly anticipates in the following passage: —

"The machinery of the new centralization is certain to be more elastic as it will be more complex, the control will be less obvious and direct; but coördination of hitherto heterogeneous elements under some predominant power is apparently as inevitable and necessary now as it was then. In comparison with the vast extent of the new system, the domain of ancient Rome shrinks to almost insignificant dimensions. The command of the habitable globe is for the first time in history possible to that power in whose hands are placed the resources that insure obedience, whose capital is the centre of exchanges. The area of its activities will embrace not Europe and the Mediterranean basin alone, but the six continents and their outlying islands; its mastership must be exercised alike in all countries."

The costs of preparation for the coming conflict are likely to be too heavy for any but the greater nations to bear. Italy and Spain are already sinking under the load of military equipments out of proportion to their resources, and France, in spite of her steadily growing wealth, is assuming heavy burdens. The French ministry, in submitting the annual estimates in January last, proposed a scale of expenditure for new naval vessels amounting to 900,000,000 francs ($175,000,000) for the period of seven years ending with 1907. Professor Paul Leroy-Beaulieu, in discussing the subject in "l'Economiste Français" of February 3, 1900, truly declares that with allowance for contingencies this scale of expenditure, if voted by the Chambers, should be considered as a round thousand millions of francs rather than nine hundred millions. He attributes this costly project to the aggressive imperialism of Great Britain in the Fachoda incident of a year ago, and declares, for the benefit of the French people, that "the only consolation, if it is one, is that England will have to expend, if the South African war continues a little longer, three or four thousand millions of francs to subjugate or leave unsubjugated two tiny republics, and that it will be necessary to increase by three or four hundred million francs at least her permanent war budget."

The German ministry has been struggling with a hesitating parliament to secure an almost equal expenditure, and the Russian Council of Ministers adopted not long ago a definite programme of naval increase extending over a period of years. The United States have lightly assumed added taxes of $100,-

000,000 a year, and their people, except in isolated cases of ill adjustment, scarcely feel the burden.

Concentration of power, in order to permit prompt and efficient action, will be an almost essential factor in the struggle for world empire, so far as the struggle is conducted in the political field. The people of the United States may have something to learn in this respect. A greater harmony of policy between the legislative and executive departments of the government, and broad powers for the executive in dealing with foreign relations, need not be inconsistent with industrial liberty and the freedom of political discussion at home. In this field an absolute government, like that of Russia, enjoys some advantages in its ability to make quick decisions and execute them without waiting for the slow ripening of public opinion. What is determined upon by the Czar and the Council of Ministers can be executed without consulting the slow processes of parliamentary legislation.

An illustration of the power which absolutism gives is afforded by the recent loan to Persia, made by direction of the Russian government on condition of the control of the Persian customs, at the moment when the difficulties of Great Britain in South Africa were most acute. It is well suggested by the "Moniteur des Intérêts Matériels," the Belgian financial journal, that neither Great Britain, in spite of her imperial policy, nor republican France, would be able to think of following such an example, and that even the German Empire drew back before the project of effective intervention on a recent occasion, — the creation of railways in the Chinese province of Shantung. But the Russian government, drawing from the limitless resources of international finance, through the medium of a new bank established in Persia, has been able, almost by the stroke of a pen and with only a trifling cost to the imperial treasury, even if the whole principal of the loan were lost, to acquire a dominant influence at the court of Teheran, which will make Persia a Russian camp in case of conflict with Great Britain over British India. Already, within a few weeks after the completion of the loan, it has been announced by a leading Russian journal that Russia will "rent" a Persian harbor (as she rented

Port Arthur from China), in order to obtain an outlet to the Indian Ocean.

In a conflict between two opposing systems, like that of organized absolutism and competitive democracy, it is the usual rule that each borrows what is best from the methods of the other. The autocracy which governs the Russian Empire appreciates the benefits of intellectual freedom sufficiently to gather around the Czar in the Council of Ministers some of the best educated, keenest, and most far-sighted minds in the world. Freedom of debate prevails in those gatherings as to the merits of proposed policies, and the Russian financial journals discuss with as much acuteness as those of any other country the economic maxims which should govern a progressive state. Thus the highest intelligence is placed at the service of absolute power, and measures are perfected and blows are struck, which rarely have to be retraced, in the field of economics or diplomacy. On the side of a progressive democracy like that of the United States, the lesson to be learned from absolutism is consolidation of kindred interests, unity of purpose, and promptness and efficiency in action. A democratic state, where education is widely diffused, ought at least to be as intelligent as a despotism in following the suggestions of its most enlightened statesmen and within the limits of national policy giving free scope to their judgment in counsel and efficiency in action.

In the field of natural resources, both the United States and Russia enjoy an important advantage over the older countries in their comparatively unexhausted coal supply. A coal famine has prevailed on the European continent during the past year, and is having a serious effect upon the industries of Germany and even of Great Britain. Coal is as vital a factor in the warfare of industries as in modern warfare on the ocean. It is not surprising, therefore, that the "Economist," in its issue of February 24, 1900, admits that "Europe's extremity is America's opportunity, and she is seizing it." Mr. Frank H. Mason, United States Consul General at Berlin, in a recent report to the State Department, declares that "Letters are received at this consulate from importers of English anthracite and gas coals, complaining of the meagre supply and high prices, and asking to be put into communication with American exporters of those grades." The export of American coal to European markets has become a recognized business, and the English journal already quoted declares that "America is now permanently established as a supplier of the foreign coaling stations."

Another vital point at which the equipment of the United States in respect to natural resources gives them a controlling advantage is in the food supply. The cultivation of great wheat areas has not been neglected in the development of manufacturing. The United States are not only self-sufficing in this respect, but by means of scientific farming upon a large scale they have been able to produce the staples of agricultural products as cheaply as any other nation. Thus, in entering upon the domain of manufacturing for world competition, they start with unexhausted fields of coal and adequate supplies of food at their elbow. They are hampered neither by the lack of proper distribution of their laboring force between manufactures and agriculture, nor by high prices of land, which tend by increasing the cost of food to raise the labor cost of production, while diminishing in other directions the consuming power of the laborer.

Turning to the field of economic and social forces, it will be seen that the United States have little to fear in the structure of their industrial system from their foreign rivals. The elements of successful industrial competition, as already pointed out, are found in the use of capital at the lowest rental price, the division of labor to that extent which secures the highest efficiency in the individual and the aggregate of individuals, the cheapest means of transportation, and the concentration of industry to just the point which secures the largest output at the smallest cost.

This list of the necessary elements for competitive production depends upon another of surpassing importance, which dominates all the rest. This is the efficiency of the directing mind, — what the French call the *entrepreneur*. It is not proposed here to discuss the question whether the *entrepreneur* under the existing organization of society obtains a disproportionate share of the earnings of labor. What is vital to a competing nation is that the rewards of his position, whether they are large or small, should be sufficient to attract the minds of the most intense application and the highest creative order. These results might perhaps be obtained while greatly diminishing the present scale of rewards and imposing heavier burdens of taxation upon accumulated wealth. But the necessity of an *entrepreneur* of the highest capacity is more vital to industrial success in the future than it has ever been in the past, when competition was shut within limited markets protected by local legislation.

It is in this field, of ability for intense application, combination of ideas, and organization upon a large scale, that the traditions of centuries of political freedom and comparative economic freedom have given supremacy to the Anglo-Saxon peoples, and especially to the Americans. With them has been realized most fully that process of social development which Mr. Kidd declares tends to raise the rivalry between individuals "to the very highest degree of efficiency as a condition of progress, by bringing all the people into it on a footing of equality, and by allowing the freest possible play of forces within the community, and the widest possible opportunities for the development of every individual's faculties and personality." It is the result of this process which makes the American people easily masters in those fields which they seriously enter. It is not surprising that the European press bristles with warnings against the manner in which our products are flooding every market. A type of these warnings, in a recent article by Mr. George Wenlersse in the "Grande Revue," is thus expressed: —

> "Gradually the Americans are pushing their way into the British colonies. The last railroad built in India has American rails. American manufacturers export their iron and motors, their machinery, and galvanic wires to Cape Colony. Egypt, too, has Philadelphia bridge builders on the scene. Three hundred railroad coaches have found their way from Jersey City into the land of the Pharaohs, and electrical tramways are forged in the foundries of Pittsburg to connect Cairo with the pyramids. Even Europe is not safe against the invasion of American goods. Russia, France, Germany, and Italy must pay tribute. England herself buys American locomotives, steel rails, paper ware, railroad coaches, and even coal. Sheffield, the home of the steel industry, has been dethroned by Pittsburg. It would be frivolity itself to remain indifferent to the expansion of this leviathan people."

Among the faculties which have enabled the American manufacturer to get a footing in these fields has been the same economy and efficiency resulting from concentration which make the larger states more potent than the smaller in the domain of world politics. It was declared before the Industrial Commission, regarding the export trade, "that it would be impossible for this trade to be secured to anything like the same extent without the power that comes from large concentration of capital in the hands of one managing body." It is not concentration alone, however, which has produced these results, but the skill with which such combinations have been handled. This is the justification of the trust, so far as it can find justification. In so far as a trust or great business enterprise has succeeded, without the control of some natural monopoly or the abuse of legislation, it has usually been the result of the superior organizing ability and foresight of its directing mind. Success has been the test of efficiency. The incompetent trust manager is driven to the wall, where competition at home or abroad is within the range of possibility, more quickly than the inefficient manager of a small trade.

The triumph of the industrial leader over his fellows, therefore, by the natural processes of competition is a direct contribution to the competing power of the nation. More and more, with the widening of the world market, the fluctuations of demand and supply, and the necessity of managing great financial operations, the captain of industry needs to possess all the genius for combination, foresight, and promptness of action which characterize the successful general in the field. As Professor Sidney Sherwood well declares in the "Yale Review" for February, 1900: —

"He must know the larger market — what its demands are and what are its sources of supply. He must possess also the ability to take broad views of the plans necessary to bring together this demand and supply. He must be a constructive statesman in industry, capable of forming large and far-reaching policies. . . .

"The undertaker must be a great engineer in economic matters, understanding how to utilize to the best advantage the highly developed skill of the laborer, the complex adjustment of the machinery, and how to combine the two.

"Finally, the vast accumulation of modern capital

and the necessity of using large capital in these productive processes make it essential for the modern *entrepreneur* to be a great financier. He must know how to get the requisite capital under his control upon advantageous terms, how to manage it economically and successfully, how to meet the payments of interest, how to avoid carrying unnecessary capital, how to preserve the confidence of the investor."

That this ability for organization is a serious factor in modern competition is coming to be generally recognized by producers and economists. Baron Mourre, in his suggestive book, "D'où Vient la Décadence Economique de la France?" cites the many proofs that French exports and French wealth are falling behind those of Germany and Great Britain in relative growth. He inquires, "What are the causes of this inferiority?" and makes this answer:—

"It is probably not that our laborers are much more incapable or more indolent than German or English workmen, but that our manufacturers direct them less efficiently and employ antiquated processes, which permit only an inadequate production."

In this respect the United States stand admittedly at the head. The organization of their great industries constitutes, as Professor Sherwood declares, "the American solution " of the problem of meeting the demands of the world market by a high type of organization. He well adds that "it is upon this historic superiority in the capacity for organization that the future economic supremacy of America must probably rest." It is in the individualism and daring, tempered by discretion, of the American industrial leader that the United States in the nature of the case surpass those peoples who are accustomed to have their thinking and acting done for them by the state. The operation of the competitive system, in forcing the ablest minds to the highest degree of exertion in order to obtain the greatest qauntum of desirable results by the smallest relative expenditure of energy, is its distinguishing advantage over the socialistic system in any of its forms. State direction of industry — useful sometimes in the infancy of technical education — and the creation of monopolies by legislation, will always give way, other conditions being equal, to the results of private industry and enterprise. No means can be found for giving to the members of a bureaucracy the motive of competitive self-interest which strains to its utmost tension the mind of the industrial chief.

The limits of state socialism are clearly marked at the point where greater efficiency ceases to be obtained on the whole by the methods of government control and ownership. Such ownership may perhaps be extended in the future to the railways and the telegraph, simply because the advantages of uniformity of system and charges and the certainty of impartiality between competitors outweigh the expensive methods of bureaucracy. But the moment that state socialism undertakes to supersede the individual initiative in enterprises which are not of a quasi-public character, the society adopting them will sentence itself to economic decline. It will no longer offer a premium to its best minds to achieve the utmost that can be achieved in improving methods of production. While at first its products may appear to compete upon equal terms with those of other nations, the gradual hardening of routine, the retention of inefficient machinery, the absence of the spur of prizes to inventors and to the captains of industry, will impair its competitive machinery, increase the cost of its product, and drive it from international markets.

If a tariff wall is erected high enough to exclude competition from abroad, such a socialistic state will gradually drop astern in the race for industrial prizes, and with growing impoverishment, the flight of foreign capital, the increasing burden of taxation, and the steady decline in the surplus available for the employment of the professional classes, the encouragement of art, and the development of the comfort of the masses, will descend lower and lower in the scale of civilization,—at first relatively to its advancing rivals, and finally absolutely in relation to its own past.

In so far as the combination of capital or labor tends to stifle reasonable competition and create monopoly, it tends to threaten the efficiency of a nation's competing power. Only upon the ground of paramount advantages in other respects can such monopoly be justified. If it be true, as declared by a critic of the Building Trades Council of Chicago, in speaking of trades-unions in Great Britain and the United States, that "the essence of trades-unionism to-day there and here is the destruction of freedom of contract and the establishment of state socialism and special privilege," this fact in itself is a serious menace to the competing power of American production. Trades-unions and combinations of labor have done much to raise the standard of living among the laboring men, to secure for labor equality of rights with capital, and thereby to increase the consuming power and the efficiency of the masses in the community. The benefits of such combinations cease when their policy and methods tend to unduly restrict producing power, to put the incompetent and slothful upon a level with the competent and energetic, and to stifle individual initiative.

If it is desirable that the supreme productive power of the best minds should be applied to industry, it is also of great importance that the rewards of industry should be as great and as honorable as those of any other calling. These rewards should be ranked by public opinion as high as those achieved in government, literature, or art. There is little danger of a conflict between commercialism and the higher ideals under such conditions, so long as the life-blood of productive energy and moral purpose flows freely from the heart to the extremities of society. There will always be a class whose members will forswear the pecuniary rewards of industrial activity for the gratifications of intellectual and artistic labor, if the surplus earnings of the community will afford them a dignified and comfortable maintenance. The process of natural selection can be trusted to divert in this direction the minds best fitted for such pursuits, while leaving to the organizing executive minds the pursuit of industrial rewards.

The greatest periods in literature and art among civilized peoples have almost always been those when they were winning victories on the field and in the workshop. It was thus with Athens in the age of Perikles and with Rome in the age of Augustus. Their intellectual life attained its highest development at the same moment with their industrial life, so far as the latter obtained a footing in ancient slaveholding societies. It was the same in the France of Louis XIV. and in the England of Elizabeth. The outburst of industrial energy and the contest for world empire were accompanied by the highest intellectual achievement and the creation of the masterpieces of the French and British drama. To the same great age which witnessed the colonization of America and the opening of India belonged the names of Turenne and Marlborough in the field, of Colbert and Bacon in constructive statesmanship, of Molière and Shakespeare in art.

The United States enter upon the field of world competition with peculiar advantages in respect to the motives which govern their intellectual development. The very complaint of many reformers, that the ablest minds neglect those official spheres once considered most honorable, for the management of factories, insurance companies, banks, and railways, is one of the results of the dignity of labor in America. It is highly desirable that the policy of the state should be well directed, and it has been pointed out that this may be an element of vital importance in the competition of our democracy with organized absolutism. But it is not desirable in a modern state that there should be a waste of forces upon the machinery of government.

It has been by the natural evolution of events that the majority in state legislatures and in Congress have ceased to be the leaders of public opinion and have become its obedient servants. Public opinion is no longer formed by debates in Congress, but by the expression of the best opinion of experts through the press. When public opinion reaches the state of decision on an important subject, it is registered more effectively by an obedient majority than would be the case if scores of experts and economists split hairs over abstractions before putting a law upon the statute book. The abstract discussion which leads to the ripening of opinion takes place outside of Congress. If more of the highest constructive and executive ability could be devoted to the service of the state, legislatures might realize a more impressive and dignified ideal than at present, but the diversion of the best minds to such a service might involve an economic waste which would react disastrously upon the real interests of the country in its competition with foreign rivals.

The people of the United States, by devoting their best talent to industry and commerce, and minimizing to some degree the honors of public service, escape another danger which impairs the competing power of their European rivals. This is the entombment of some of the highest capacity of the country in the barren service of arms. It is absolutely essential that every nation should be able to protect its independence and its national interests in the struggle for commercial empire, which may cause many appeals to arms in the future. But that nation which is able to maintain its military efficiency with the smallest possible subtraction from its resources for industrial development will be the strongest competitor for the empire of arts as well as arms.

It is not perhaps the most serious fetter upon the competitive power of the European countries that their people give up a large part of their earnings for the military establishment. This can be afforded without suffering by the richer nations, in view of the greatly increased productive power of the race under modern conditions. As Professor Edmond Théry points out, in "l'Economiste Européen," of January 19, 1900, an increase of 97 per cent. in the taxes collected from the people of France between 1869 and 1898, while the population remained nearly stationary, has been accompanied by great improvements in public education, in asylums, in institutions of philanthropy and coöperation, and the wages of labor have risen from 50 to 60 per cent. above their average a generation ago. But in this same France, in spite of her industry and accumulated wealth, the persistence of the feudal idea that trade is ignoble and idleness alone honorable contributes even to-day, in the opinion of Baron Mourre, in the work already quoted, to her steady decline in competition with other industrial nations. "The French," he says, "instead of developing their capital themselves, invest in securities and struggle for petty official places." The fatal defect of the policy of militarism, which is gnawing at the vitals of the continental states of Europe, is not the direct cost in money, but the persistence of the mediæval idea that the display of gold lace or the bearing of civil titles is more honorable than distinction in the fields of industry. It is this idea which shuts up the keenest and most ambitious minds in the narrow treadmill of official routine or military ostentation, and withdraws them from their truest service to humanity.

Of transcendent importance also in the struggle for industrial supremacy is the keeping open to all classes of the paths which lead to the highest industrial rewards. It was one of the misfortunes of the Roman state that trade and industry were treated as unfit for freemen, as they are disparaged to-day in the military courts of Europe and among the parvenu aristocracy which apes foreign customs in this country. But a deeper evil than this was the stratification of society. Among the genuine Romans, especially under the Empire, social classes hardened into castes, and the ablest and most ambitious minds could find no escape from the class into which they had been born. Mr. Dill, in his interesting work on "Roman Society in the Last Century of the Western Empire," sets forth in striking language the manner in which the carriers of grain from Sicily, Spain, and Egypt to Rome, and the various city traders, were shut within their class, and how completely the food service of the city broke down when it was no longer in the power of the state to maintain this forced stratification of society.

It is no new discovery on the part of Mr.

Dill that this binding of classes by iron barriers was the canker which gnawed at the life of the Roman state. It is the testimony of Mommsen, the great German historian of Rome, and of Léon, in his "Histoire des Corporations de Métiers." "The craftsman," says the latter, "was riveted to his trade like the convict to his chain. Nothing in theory could withdraw him from this yoke; the Emperor himself was forbidden from granting him release." Every industry was organized into guilds, and in some cases a man could not marry the daughter of a craftsman without being compelled to adopt his father-in-law's trade. It is not surprising that under such a system, where, in the language of Mr. Dill, "law, sentiment, the course of events, were hostile to the prosperity of a great commercial class," merchants should have fled from the great centres of commerce, with the object of escaping the special taxes on their calling; nor is it surprising that under such conditions of embyro state socialism the Roman state, decaying at the top, lost its vitality, and when the barriers of caste were finally broken down by the rude swords of Goths and Vandals, there were, as Gibbon so tersely says, "no longer any proper Romans left to defend her."

A similar experience was that of Athens, where her robust democracy, gradually stratified into rigid classes, died at the top and fell before the vigorous march of the soldiers of Macedon. In France, it was the great mistake of Colbert that he strove to organize the people into classes, and to give a fictitious splendor to French industry by conferring the privileges of monopoly on a few showy manufactures. The guilds or corporations came to impose unbearable fetters upon the life of French industry, and contributed their share to the impoverishment which was sinking interior France to the level of barbarism, while wealth and wit shone resplendent at the courts of Louis XIV. and Louis XV. As Taine interprets the observation of Arthur Young, who traversed the country just before the Revolution, never was there a society with "a heart so vigorous and extremities so benumbed."

Such a society could not live to-day in competition with a democratic industrial commonwealth, where equality of burdens and equality of opportunity afford the strongest stimulus to the activity of the race by offering the highest prizes to the greatest achievement. Turgot only anticipated the effect of the relentless competition of modern times when he tried to abolish the corporations and to open to every Frenchman the pathway for seeking his own future in his own way, before the blood of the Revolution swept away social and political distinctions in France and enabled her to stand forth, in spite of the frightful drain of Napoleon's campaigns, as a competitor of modern industrial nations. If England was already the leader in this competition, and France lagged behind, it was largely, as Mr. Hobson declares in "The Evolution of Modern Capitalism," because "she, more than any other European nation, had broken down the old industrial order, with its guilds, its elaborate restrictions, and conservative methods. Personal freedom, security of property, liberty to work and live where and how one liked, existed in England to an extent unknown on the continent."

It is a well-settled rule of social development that any society which has ceased to feel the spur of need and ambition has begun to decay. The man who has become rich ceases to devote the same relentless energy and minute care to his business as when he was poor. Even if hardened habits keep him at the treadmill, his children are bred in a different school, and are only rarely his efficient successors in the fields of finance and industry. Even if every one of them were so, the statistics of births and deaths show that the upper class in any fixed society steadily declines in number in ratio to the lower classes, and finally dies out. Only when new blood is constantly poured into the so-called "upper" grades of society from beneath, or into the city from the country, does their vitality remain unimpaired, and only under such conditions can a people go forward in the field of industry, of art, and of world empire from victory unto victory. The attempt to stratify society, — whether it comes from above or beneath, whether it is in the interest of a blooded or moneyed aristocracy, of organized labor or of socialism, — is to put the bar sinister upon national life and sentence a state to fall gradually behind in the race for commercial and political empire, until she sinks a helpless prey to her more democratic and vigorous rivals.

Painful as it may be to patrician prejudices, it is the constant change in social classification — the success of the new-comers, the decay of old families — which keeps the lifeblood of a nation flowing freely from the heart to the extremities. In the words quoted by Professor Leroy-Beaulieu, in his "Traité d'Economie Politique," "One hears constantly the sound of polished boots descending, of wooden shoes mounting upward." Upon this subject nothing can be truer than the conclusion at which Mr. Benjamin Kidd arrived in the closing pages of his profound study on "Social Evolution:" —

"Under all the complex appearances our Western civilization presents, the central process working itself out in our midst is one which is ever tending to bring, for the first time in the history of the race, all the people into the competition of life on a footing of equality of opportunity. In this process the problem, with which society and legislators will be concerned for long into the future, will be how to secure to the fullest degree these conditions of equality, while at the same time retaining that degree of inequality which must result from offering prizes sufficiently attractive to keep up within the community that state of stress and exertion, without which no people can long continue in a high state of social efficiency."

To the Anglo-Saxon race, by the historical evolution of events, has been committed this cause of modern social progress. Imperfectly as they may have conceived it, clumsily and with much travail as they may perform it, it is a task which they cannot escape unless the world is to sink backward into another long night like that of the Dark Ages. It is a mission of the highest altruism, in which commercial and economic forces play a part only because economic efficiency is the fruit of freedom, and the people of the highest moral ideals are those capable of doing the most in the world. The function of the highly developed peoples, as Professor Walter F. Willcox pointed out at a recent meeting of the Washington Economic Society, is to teach labor-saving devices and efficient methods of production to the less advanced peoples, to the end that every part of the world may yield its increase in the largest measure for humanity. In pursuance of this work, it is not the duty of the Anglo-Saxon races to force their policies by the sword upon reluctant rivals, but it is their duty to accept without regret or turning back the responsibilities which come to them, and to insist that the policies of absolutism and exclusion shall not usurp fields where free competition and equality of opportunity now prevail or may reasonably be established.

The position of the United States as a factor in international politics makes it more important than in her earlier history that she should pursue a continuous and resolute diplomatic policy. A resolute policy does not by any means imply the sort of hysterical bullying which has sometimes marked our attitude toward weaker nations, but simply a firm insistence upon respect for American rights, and the readiness to sustain these rights, if necessary, by force. The struggle for the maintenance of free markets and equality of opportunity in the undeveloped countries will involve tactful diplomacy, firmness tempered by extreme discretion, and readiness to act promptly and efficiently in case of need. The United States can no longer afford to have an amateur consular and diplomatic service, nor to have it suspected that their policy will change with the change of parties at home. That party will most commend itself to the business community for its sincerity as the advocate of extending our national influence and competing power which does the most to increase the efficiency of the consular and diplomatic service by lifting it out of politics. In this direction, as in all others, the highest efficiency will turn the scale between nations, and this efficiency is usually won in diplomacy, as in the technical arts, by training and knowledge.

At the most critical moments, the political party which represents a well-formulated and resolute policy will command the support of those who believe in the maintenance of the position of the United States as a world power. This will not preclude changes of political control, and there will no doubt be moments when discontent with the party of a constructive policy will place its opponents in office. It is of the highest importance, however, that the interests of the country should be intrusted as largely as possible to that party which has a well-defined policy, and that, if its power is to be relinquished at intervals, the demand should at least be made by the people that the broadest and most constructive statesmen of the opposition party should be placed in control of foreign affairs.

These intervals of the success of the parliamentary opposition should be limited, as far as possible, to periods of arrested progress rather than absolute retrogression. Great Britain encountered such periods under the timid policy of Mr. Gladstone, but even he was forced by events to assume a protectorate for Great Britain over Egypt and to do other things as a responsible minister which would have invited his philippics if he had enjoyed the freedom of an opposition leader. But England is coming to understand how vital is the maintenance of her position before the world, and how completely settled are some of the old issues which once divided parties. In the United States also, the old issues are shriveling up, — settled and sent to the lumber-room of the political theatre, or tinged with strange, new light by the flash of Dewey's guns in the Bay of Manila. Events are opening the way for party divisions upon new issues, in which the party of a continuous national policy, pledged to keep open the world market upon conditions of equal opportunity, will command the support not alone of the business community, but of all far-seeing men who desire the perpetuation of the ideals of Anglo-Saxon civilization.

The great Republic of the West, in girding her loins for this struggle, should so direct her policy that if she is compelled to draw the sword, it should not be to enforce the privileges of classes, but on behalf of the essential mission of democracy, — equality of opportunity for all, — and as the champion of the civilization of the future in the realization of its highest ideals. If this contest should bear something of the character of that between Persia and Greece of old, our race, by its training in representative government, has at least learned how to guard against the fatal divisions which made the Greek cities of Asia a prey to Darius and Xerxes, and how to confront the organized forces of absolutism and trade exclusion by the united democracy of America. For this great industrial empire, the sword must ever be a last resort, unsheathed only in behalf of the freedom and civilization of the world, in accordance with that maxim of subtle wisdom blazoned on the seal of Massachusetts, "*Ense petit placidam sub libertate quietem*," — "By the sword she seeks gentle peace under the shield of liberty."

LIST OF PERIODICALS

FROM WHICH THE CHAPTERS OF THIS BOOK WERE TAKEN,

WITH THE CONSENT OF THE PUBLISHERS.

The Economic Basis of Imperialism, *North American Review*, September, 1898, clxvii. p. 326.

Russia as a World Power, *North American Review*, February, 1899, clxviii. p. 178.

The Struggle for Commercial Supremacy, *The Forum*, June, 1899, xxvii. p. 427.

Can New Openings be found for Capital? *The Atlantic Monthly*, November, 1899, lxxxiv. p. 600.

The New Economic Problems (printed under the title, "Recent Economic Tendencies"), *The Atlantic Monthly*, June, 1900, lxxxv. p. 737.

The United States as a World Power — The Economic and Political Problem, *The Forum*, July, 1900, xxix. p. 608.

The United States as a World Power — Their Advantages in the Competition for Commercial Empire, *The Forum*, August, 1900, xxix. p. 673.

INDEX

INDEX